T0270641

Disrupting Journalism Ethics

Disrupting Journalism Ethics sets out to disrupt and change how we think about journalism and its ethics. The book contends that long-established ways of thinking, which have come down to us from the history of journalism, need radical conceptual reform, with alternate conceptions of the role of journalism and fresh principles to evaluate practice. Through a series of disruptions, the book undermines the traditional principles of journalistic neutrality and "just the facts" reporting. It proposes an alternate philosophy of journalism as engagement for democracy. The aim is a journalism ethic better suited to an age of digital and global media.

As a philosophical pragmatist, Stephen J. A. Ward critiques traditional conceptions of accuracy, neutrality, detachment, and patriotism, evaluating their capacity to respond to ethical dilemmas for journalists in the 21st century. The book proposes a holistic mindset for doing journalism ethics, a theory of journalism as advocacy for egalitarian democracy, and a global redefinition of basic journalistic norms. The book concludes by outlining the shape of a future journalism ethics, employing these alternative notions.

Disrupting Journalism Ethics is an important intervention into the role of journalism today. It asks: what new role *should* journalists play in today's digital media world? And what new mindset, new aims, and new standards *ought* journalists to embrace? Its aim is to persuade – and provoke – ethicists, journalists, students, and members of the public to disrupt and invent.

Stephen J. A. Ward is an internationally recognized media ethicist, author, and educator. He is Distinguished Lecturer in Ethics at the University of British Columbia, founding director of the Center for Journalism Ethics at the University of Wisconsin, USA, and former director of the Graduate School of Journalism at the University of British Columbia. He was a war correspondent, foreign reporter, and newsroom manager for 14 years and has received a lifetime award for service to professional journalism in Canada. Ward is the author of nine books on journalism and media ethics, including *The Invention of Journalism Ethics* (2006) and the award-winning *Radical Media Ethics* (2015).

Disruptions: Studies in Digital Journalism
Series editor: Bob Franklin

Disruptions refers to the radical changes provoked by the affordances of digital technologies that occur at a pace and on a scale that disrupts settled understandings and traditional ways of creating value, interacting and communicating both socially and professionally. The consequences for digital journalism involve far reaching changes to business models, professional practices, roles, ethics, products and even challenges to the accepted definitions and understandings of journalism. For Digital Journalism Studies, the field of academic inquiry which explores and examines digital journalism, disruption results in paradigmatic and tectonic shifts in scholarly concerns. It prompts reconsideration of research methods, theoretical analyses and responses (oppositional and consensual) to such changes, which have been described as being akin to 'a moment of mind blowing uncertainty'.

Routledge's new book series, *Disruptions: Studies in Digital Journalism*, seeks to capture, examine and analyse these moments of exciting and explosive professional and scholarly innovation which characterize developments in the day-to-day practice of journalism in an age of digital media, and which are articulated in the newly emerging academic discipline of Digital Journalism Studies.

Native Advertising
Lisa Lynch

Geographies of Journalism
The Imaginative Power of Place in Making Digital News
Robert E Gutsche Jr. and Kristy Hess

Disrupting Journalism Ethics
Radical Change on the Frontier of Digital Media
Stephen J. A. Ward

For more information about this series, please visit: www.routledge.com/Disruptions/book-series/DISRUPTDIGJOUR

Disrupting Journalism Ethics

Radical Change on the Frontier
of Digital Media

Stephen J. A. Ward

LONDON AND NEW YORK

First published 2019 by Routledge

2 Park Square, Milton Park, Abingdon, Oxon OX14 4RN
605 Third Avenue, New York, NY 10017

Routledge is an imprint of the Taylor & Francis Group, an informa business

First issued in paperback 2021

Publisher's Note

The publisher has gone to great lengths to ensure the quality of this reprint
but points out that some imperfections in the original copies may be apparent.

British Library Cataloguing-in-Publication Data
A catalogue record for this book is available from the British Library

Library of Congress Cataloging-in-Publication Data
Names: Ward, Stephen J. A. (Stephen John Anthony), 1951– author.
Title: Disrupting journalism ethics : radical change on the frontier
   of digital media / Stephen J. A. Ward.
Description: London ; New York : Routledge, 2019. | Series:
   Disruptions: studies in digital journalism | Includes
   bibliographical references and index.
Identifiers: LCCN 2018025193 | Subjects: LCSH: Journalistic
   ethics. | Online journalism. | Ethics.
Classification: LCC PN4756 .W365 2019 | DDC 174/.907—dc23
LC record available at https://lccn.loc.gov/2018025193

ISBN: 978-1-138-89574-4 (hbk)
ISBN: 978-1-03-217858-5 (pbk)
DOI: 10.4324/9781315179377

Typeset in Times New Roman
by Apex CoVantage, LLC

To Nadia, for disrupting my life

Contents

Figures

1 Why disrupt?

This book examines how we think about journalism, and how to change it. It asks: what new role *should* journalists play in today's digital media world? What new mindset, new aims, and new standards *ought* journalists to embrace?

The italicized words – *should, ought* – indicate that this is a book about journalism ethics. Journalism ethics is not difficult to define. Journalism ethics is the responsible use of the freedom to publish; it is the study and application of the norms that should guide responsible, public journalism. That is the easy part. The hard part is saying what "responsible" means in general – what principles and stances? – and, what it means in particular – how to apply these norms to complex situations in daily journalism. Saying what the ethics of journalism should be is doubly difficult because of rapidly changing media, new practitioners, new values, and new practices. Today, journalism ethics is a *problem*, a zone of contention.

Why start with how we think? Because, as a philosophical pragmatist, I am interested in the consequences of beliefs, i.e., how we think and arrive at decisions, and what difference that makes in the world. To trace the consequences, one must be able to identify the beliefs. One must be a philosophical "detective," noting that certain ideas are at work below the surface of our actions and thinking, as unstated assumptions.

The hypothesis

The general hypothesis of the book is that journalism ethics needs radical conceptual reform – alternate conceptions of the role of journalism and fresh principles to evaluate practice. These new ideas need to be brought together into a comprehensive perspective that explains what responsible journalism means in a digital, media world. The hypothesis contends that long-established ways of thinking, which have come down to us from the history of journalism, need to be disrupted and replaced by better ways of thinking. Strict adherence to traditional perspectives discourages bolder thinking and the development of new models.

The ethical problems cannot be properly addressed by minor reformulation of existing precepts. No doubt, after reform, some major principles will remain, such as truth-telling and verification, but even those that remain will have to be reinterpreted and reapplied to current issues. Reform will fail if it occurs in a piecemeal, *ad hoc* manner, modifying a norm here and responding to a problem there. We need to dig deep, intellectually. The future of journalism ethics depends on creative thinkers who *overcome* entrenched ways of thinking through critique and new proposals. We need to throw off the weight of journalistic tradition. It is time to be philosophically radical, to rethink journalism ethics from the ground up.

To support the hypothesis, I need to do two large things in this book: (1) to say what those long-established ways of thinking are, and why they need to be critiqued and (2) to say what a new journalism ethics should look like. In the rest of this Introduction, I orientate the reader by explaining why we need to disrupt and by sketching the argument to come.

When disrupt?

To morally interpret a practice is to explain the point of the practice. The point is the ethical aim of the practice, e.g., the way that law aims at justice and medicine aims at health of the body. As Dworking states: "A participant interpreting a social practice . . . proposes a value for the practice by describing some scheme of interests or goals or principles the practice can be taken to serve or express or exemplify."[1]

A moral interpretation is a moral ideology. By ideology, I mean a system of ideas that help us to understand, accurately or inaccurately, some object or activity in the world.[2] There are political, moral, economic, and religious ideologies. Ideologies are practical. They are intended to be used for guiding conduct. A moral ideology for journalism is a system of aims and norms that guide conduct according to some view of the point of the practice – the practice at its best. The history of journalism is redolent with moral interpretations: the journalist as neutral reporter of facts; the journalist as reformer or revolutionary; the journalist as the elixir of democracy.

To disrupt journalism ethics, then, is to disrupt one or more of the dominant moral ideologies of journalism. One disrupts the normal functioning of a moral ideology by questioning its goals, challenging its value judgments, exposing its dubious assumptions, showing how ineffective the ideology is in guiding decisions, and by offering an alternate interpretation.

Disruption has two related parts, like two sides of a coin: deconstruction and reconstruction. Deconstruction is the analytical task of taking moral ideologies of journalism apart and critiquing their component ideas. Reconstruction is the synthetic task of putting ideas together to form an alternate moral view.

Disruption is not always necessary. There are skills, such as plumbing or flying airplanes, where it would be out of place to call for an intellectual revolution and a new ideology. Even in highly intellectual activities, such as science, there is a time for major reform and a time when it is not needed. Historian of science Thomas Kuhn said the sciences alternate between "normal" and "revolutionary" periods.[3] During normal science, most scientists agree on the basic methods, aims, and theories of their discipline. At other times, disagreement arises, and a lack of consensus on fundamentals prevails. New ideas come forward. The science enters a revolutionary period. Many things can undermine consensus, such as the emergence of a major new theory, new practices, new instruments, and failed experiments.

How do we know when a dominant moral ideology of journalism has been undermined and journalism ethics has entered a revolutionary period? When two things happen: (a) the main ideas of the ideology are disputed, rejected, or ignored in practice; there is serious fragmentation in ethical belief and (b) the ideology is not useful in addressing new practices and new problems, especially during times of rapid change. In sum, an ideology is in trouble when it struggles to be a widely respected, effective normative guide for practice. At this point, disruption is a valid option.

Why disrupt now?

I advocate disruption because the field of journalism ethics, overall, satisfies the conditions noted above. Journalism ethics has switched from normal to revolutionary mode. Disagreement is widespread, and there is a lack of consensus on fundamentals such as the primary aim of journalism. Historically, we are in the fifth revolution in journalism ethics since the creation of the modern news press in 17th-century Europe.[4]

What is the primary cause of this fragmentation? It is the digital media revolution, a revolution in media of unprecedented proportions. The revolution consists of three large factors: (1) the rise of digital media allowing citizens to publish and practice journalism, far from the professional newsrooms where journalism ethics began; (2) the rise of extreme populism and intolerant groups empowered by technologies that spread misinformation, polluting the public sphere; and (3) a global public sphere. News media are now global in reach, impact, and content as they report on global issues or events, whether the issue is immigration, climate change, or international security.

All three factors create turmoil in the ethics of journalism and weaken traditional values.

First, accessible digital media means new forms of journalism and new practitioners with varied values and aims. Citizens have access to publishing technology that can "do" journalism in two ways: citizens can regularly or randomly commit "acts of journalism" by posting information on events or commenting on issues. Or, they can use the techniques of journalism, e.g., dramatic narratives and images, to promote whatever cause they support. Many of these media workers lack knowledge of existing principles of journalism or care little for ethics; or, they assert that they work according to their own, and different, values.

Today, there is barely a principle or aim that goes unquestioned. New forms of journalism can be emotive and perspectival, and openly partisan. Traditional concepts, such as news objectivity and neutrality, are rejected. New areas of practice call for new ethical norms, such as norms for participatory journalism – where citizens are part of the news process.

When the aims of journalism are raised, a plurality of kinds of journalist are up for discussion. In addition to objective reporters, there are online opinion journalists; fiercely partisan journalists; civic-minded, engaged journalists; citizen-inclusive "participatory" journalists; and social media journalists. All have different aims. To make matters worse, this disagreement occurs at the worst possible time – when journalists seek agreement on norms for new tools, from the ethics of social media to the responsible use of technologies such as crowdsourcing, drones, and virtual reality. The result, ethically, is fragmentation. Journalism ethics is so fragmented that it resembles an archipelago of separate islands of value, where journalists hold different and incommensurable interpretations of what journalism ought to be.

Second, responsible journalists now work in a toxic (and global) public sphere of partisan media content, misinformation, hackers and trolls, political networks, extreme populists, and far-right "journalism." To counter these worldwide forces, it is not sufficient that journalists define themselves in traditional terms – reporting events and alleged facts in a neutral and balanced manner. A fundamental rethinking of journalism's primary aims is required.

Third, the globalization of news media questions the historically dominant view that journalists are, first and foremost, patriotic to their nation. The duties of journalism ethics are parochial – to the citizens of a nation. But in a global media world, should journalism ethics stop at one's border? If stories with serious impact cross borders, what are the ethical norms for evaluating their publication? What the larger and different duties of global news media? Do we need to refashion journalism ethics as a global media ethics?

Shifting issues

To appreciate how the issues for journalism ethics have changed, compare a list of the issues that have been taught in journalism ethics courses for years with a list of the new issues of digital news media. Traditionally, the problem areas have been:

- *accuracy and verification*: How much verification and context is required to publish a story? How much editing and "gate-keeping" is necessary?
- *independence and allegiances*: How can journalists be independent but maintain ethical relations with their employers, editors, advertisers, sources, the police, and the public? When is a journalist too close to a source or in a conflict of interest?
- *deception and fabrication*: Should journalists misrepresent themselves or use recording technology, such as hidden cameras, to get a story? Should literary journalists invent dialogue or create composite "characters"?
- *graphic images and image manipulation*: When should journalists publish graphic or gruesome images? When do published images constitute sensationalism or exploitation? When and how should images be altered?
- *sources and confidentiality*: Should journalists promise confidentiality to sources? How far does that protection extend? Should journalists go "off the record"?
- *special situations*: How should journalists report hostage-takings, major breaking news, suicide attempts, and other events where coverage could exacerbate the problem? When should journalists violate privacy?

Here, in contrast, are some of the issues that dominate digital journalism ethics:

- *questions of identity*: If citizens and non-professional journalists report and analyze events around the world, who is a journalist?
- *questions about scope*: If everyone is potentially a publisher, does journalism ethics apply to everyone? If so, how does that change the nature and teaching of journalism ethics?
- *questions about content*: What are the most appropriate principles, approaches, and purposes for digital journalism ethics? For example, is news objectivity still a valid ideal?
- *questions about new journalism*: How can new forms of journalism, e.g. non-profit journalism or entrepreneurial journalism, maintain standards such as editorial independence?
- *questions about community engagement*: What ethical norms should guide the use of citizen content and newsroom partnerships with external groups?
- *questions about global impact*: Should journalists see themselves as global communicators? How do journalists reconcile their patriotic

values with their duty to humanity and to address global issues from multiple perspectives?

• *questions about amplification of intolerant voices and fake news*: How should journalists cover the actions of intolerant groups and avoid being the purveyors of false facts and fake news?

The difference between the two lists is not that traditional concerns, e.g., editorial independence or anonymous sources, have disappeared. They have not. The difference is otherwise and threefold: one, the discussion of traditional concerns in the past presumed relatively wide agreement on the journalism principles that would adjudicate any specific issue. No such consensus exists today. Two, even where the issue is the same, e.g., verifying stories, the context and problems are different. Verification in a digital world is different from the traditional and, by comparison, "leisurely" pace of verifying stories for tomorrow's newspaper. Third, the new list goes deeper and asks questions about the nature and aims of journalism.

What consensus? The professional model

Talk of fragmentation of an existing ethic and the rejection of traditional principles leads to the question: what was the field of journalism ethics *before* the digital revolution?

Given that journalism is a multi-nation enterprise, it would be foolhardy to claim that there was one ethical model observed by most or all journalists. Journalists will never totally agree on their ethics, and diversity in practice is a good thing, overall. Nevertheless, there are dominant *traditions* and principles in journalism amid the diversity, allowing for some useful, if qualified, generalizations. One has only to compare the hundreds of journalism codes of ethics to see agreement on certain principles, such as truth-seeking and accuracy.[5]

My generalization is this: beginning in the early 20th century, in Western journalism, particularly in North America and Western Europe, journalism ethics changed from an idiosyncratic, newsroom-specific set of informal rules to a codified, craft-wide set of explicit principles for the new professional journalists. The codes applied to all journalists of a certain type (e.g., broadcasters) or to all journalists in a nation. The codes constituted a professional model of responsible journalism. There emerged a consensus that, at a minimum, journalism ethics meant a commitment to factual truth-telling in an objective manner. The principles for news reporting included neutrality, accuracy, pre-publication verification, the separation of news and opinion, and editorial independence. The same principles were not applied, or applied with less vigor, to editorial commentary and opinion.[6] The rationale for these principles was political: this was the type of journalism that best promoted democracy, by providing accurate, unbiased information to citizens. This modern journalism ethics was created and controlled by the ranks of professional journalists toiling in newsrooms for what we now call the "legacy" mainstream news media, such familiar entities as CNN, the BBC, the *New York Times*, Reuters news service, the *Toronto Star*, *Time* magazine, NBC news, and so on.

The consensus, of course, was never unanimous and uniform. Provisions in codes were interpreted differently by individual journalists and news outlets. Media cultures stressed some principles more than others. For example, professionals in North America stressed neutrality and reporting "just the facts," while their European colleagues tended to prefer reporting facts from within some political perspective. However, in general, the principles of objectivity, pre-publication verification, accuracy, and so on, were dominant. They populated countless codes of journalism ethics and formed the basis for innumerable books and ethics lectures. By the 1930s, these principles and aims were a dominant moral ideology for professional, mainstream journalism.[7]

It was *this* ideology, and *this* consensus, that would be challenged by the digital media revolution. The ideology would undergo criticism from many groups throughout the 1900s.[8] But the fatal blow to its preeminence would come when the digital revolution placed the powers of mass publication and communication in the hands of citizens.

Why did journalists construct this model? A professional ethics began to emerge as the new mass commercial press of the late 1800s turned journalism into a business of news. This press had come to enjoy a virtual monopoly on the provision of news, analysis, and advertising to the public. The public became passive consumers of information dependent on data provided by a professional class of journalists employed by large news organizations. In the early 1900s and beyond, this dependency raised public concerns about the reliability of this mediating class of news workers. Did the press really serve the public, or did it advance its own interests? Did it tell the truth, or was it biased? Critics charged the press with being sensationalistic, occupied by the trivial, biased by its major advertisers, and directed by powerful press barons.[9]

Journalists responded by creating the field of modern journalism ethics, as a practical set of norms for newsroom practice. Journalists in the USA and elsewhere established professional associations. The associations constructed codes of ethics with the aforementioned principles. The principles would be developed into an elaborate set of newsroom rules to ensure that journalists reported factually and objectively.[10] This self-imposed ethics, supported by accountability structures such as press councils and readers' ombudsmen, would constitute the self-regulation of journalism. In the final analysis, professionalism and objectivity were meant to assure a skeptical public that journalists would use their power to publish responsibly, and to ward off government regulation.

Out of sync

A number of the model's principles and aims remain valid and important, such as its support for democracy and editorial independence. It is difficult to imagine an ethical model that did not affirm verification and accuracy. Yet, in retrospect, we can see that the model would not be in sync with much of the online journalism as it made its appearance in the late 20th century. Especially out of sync was the moral interpretation of the model, which told reporters to remain neutral and not insert their views into stories. Journalists should coolly report on the political rivalry among groups; they do not join any of the groups. They report on advocates, but they do not advocate. To interpret or advocate is to express a bias. This view of journalism would not sit well with the perspectival journalism that became popular online by the end of the 1900s. Nevertheless, this professional framework remains influential. When the USA-based Society of Professional Journalists (SPJ) revised their code in 2014, the approach to journalism remained that of the journalist as impartial reporter.

Why do I believe that journalism ethics, rooted in this model, needs major reform?

The quick answer is that it was an ethic developed by a different news media for a different media era. Conditions change, and so do ethics. The fashioners of this traditional ethic, beginning in the early 1900s, provided normative guidance for an emerging class of professional journalists working mainly for newspapers in a non-global world. They could not envisage the issues that would face today's responsible practice. They did not write norms for a hybrid journalism of professionals and citizens, and their ever evolving forms of journalism.

To be specific, the model needs major reform because it is ineffective in addressing ethical issues arising from the three factors driving the media revolution.

With regard to new forms of journalism, the model, due to its opposition to perspective in reporting, provides little guidance on what norms should guide interpretive journalism, nor can it guide forms of journalism that regard the journalist as engaged. Moreover, the model's principles struggle to apply to new practices and problems. Take, for example, pre-publication verification. As mentioned, how does the idea of time-consuming, rigorous verification of all facts apply to news media in an era of rapid sharing of information? What does it say about the idea that the "crowd" (readers online) can correct or verify stories *after* posting? What does accuracy mean in an era of live-blogging events, of quickly incorporating data from social media on breaking stories, and of using "user-generated content" (data from citizens)? What does editorial independence mean, and how is it protected, when journalists openly declare their support for political groups or ideologies; and new types of newsrooms, such as non-profit investigative newsrooms, rely directly on funding from institutes and citizens? What new ethical thinking is needed to responsibly use new tools for journalism, such as using "big data" methods, using drones for news coverage, and using virtual reality to tell more arresting narratives?

I do not question accuracy, verification, truth-telling or independence as general principles. But I do think the model's interpretation of those principles, given its ideology of neutral fact-reporting, is either hostile to the interpretive-perspectival approach of new practices, or it struggles to apply its principles to the problems of digital media. At the very least, a serious reinterpretation and "extension" of principles are in order. Go back to the list of new issues in journalism and ask yourself: does the model have much that is relevant and useful do say about the many new problems? My view is no, it does not. This is not because someone has not taken the time to extend the model to new areas of practice. The difficulty is deeper: the model's approach is, in large part, incompatible with emerging approaches. The model lacks the conceptual resources to turn itself into an effective ethic for new journalism.

On the toxic nature of the public sphere, the professional model, with its notion of reporters as non-engaged reporters of (alleged) fact, is singularly unsuited to deal with the misinformation of extreme populists and partisan groups. As I will argue, in an ideologically divided public sphere, journalists should be active, critical interpreters engaged in the protection and advocacy of egalitarian democracy. And *that* is a form of non-neutral journalism which the traditional model typically regards with suspicion, as subjective or biased. As I will argue in the next chapter, the suspicion is based on a discredited, dualistic epistemology of journalism.

Finally, with respect to media globalization, the parochial, nation-based approach of the traditional model cannot properly guide a global journalism and the reporting of global issues. What is needed, as I discuss in Chapter 4, is a radical revision of journalism ethics so that its aims and principles are based on global, not parochial, values.

If you suspect I am exaggerating the impact of this revolutionary period, conduct this thought experiment. Imagine yourself as a journalism ethicist appearing in court as an expert witness. The case involves a company suing a media outlet for unethical practices harmful to the plaintiff. What code of ethics, or what model of journalism, will you use to ground your judgments? Assume you pick the traditional code of the Society of Professional Journalists. Under cross-examination, you are asked: do all professional journalists subscribe to this code? Do all media workers, professional or not, agree on your code? Are there other codes, such as the new online codes, that differ from your code? The SPJ embraces an impartial, non-engaged journalism, but what about citizen journalists, and engaged media writers? Does your favored code apply to them? If the defendant is the operator of their own blog or an online web site, and does not claim to be a professional journalist, is he or she bound by your code? What if he or she follows a different set of values?

Tough questions.

My point is not that there is no such thing as journalism ethics, or everything in ethics is relative. My point is that the fragmentation of journalism ethics raises questions about the legitimate application of any code when serious controversy erupts. The media revolution makes defensible responses to these questions more difficult than when there was a professional consensus on principles. Ethics today is not so tidy.

However, despite the need for change, there are people who do not think reform needs to be radical. I have been told by conservative-minded scholars, editors, and ethicists that we do not need a new ethics. It is a just a matter of "pouring new wine into old bottles." "New wine" refers to new forms of journalism. "Old bottles" refers to existing principles. I disagree. We need new bottles.

To speak of journalism ethics today is to speak in the future and normative tense. What should journalism ethics look like, in the not too distant future? The question is not how do we dig in and defend traditional principles. The task is not to circle the proverbial wagons to protect journalism ethics from the "barbarians" using media today. The question is what new ethic can guide responsible media practitioners in a chaotic, ever-expanding media universe. If we are attuned properly to this media revolution, to its deep implications for humanity and communication, our ethics discourse and our ethics work will, perforce, have a sharp edge.

The continuing influence

Some people may think that the professional model I describe belongs to the past. That I am concerning myself with a faded ideology. Is not today's reporting among mainstream news media more tolerant about interpretation and perspectives? Do not journalists today doubt the idea of objectivity?

This is true. Journalism practice has evolved. Yet the objective model continues to influence how a significant number of newsrooms operate, and the content of codes of ethics. Also, the model still shapes how we discuss journalism – especially how to move into the future. Rarely a day goes by without some story on journalism ethics citing a newsroom editor or commentator on the need for journalists to stick to facts, or public complaints that the news media is biased and not objective. Despite changes in reporting, we lack a coherent, theoretical model to justify the new interpretive journalism, and we lack clear norms by which to differentiate between good and bad forms of perspective journalism.

The model of news objectivity is based on philosophical dualisms of fact versus opinion and neutrality versus engagement which have a long cultural history. These ways of thinking have infiltrated our thinking at so many levels that we can scarce think of other ideas of objectivity. Even though academics today reject the dualism, the dualisms continue to be part of our everyday thinking. Here are the main dualistic ideas that never died: (1) the idea that facts can be scrubbed clean and become pure encapsulated facts; (2) a strict, neutral attitude that, through numbers and machines, can eliminate the bias of the human inquirer; (3) a strict division between observation and everything else we know; and (4) a fact-value dualism as the default position of people when they discuss morals. Until we dig up the roots of these concepts, we will be tempted to maintain the dualisms in whole or in part.

Similarly, we cannot overcome the model in journalism by superficial analysis, e.g., rejecting, without solid argument, the idea of objectivity as passé. The model cannot be defeated by a fashionable skepticism of objectivity. The model is rooted in the collective experiences of many journalists in the past. It helped journalism overcome a prior model – the idea of politically partisan newspapers. In the early 1900s, when the public was demanding better information, the model helped to develop a more reliable journalism. Moreover, the model affirms values that still ring true: that journalists should not let their biases or attachments compromise the truthfulness or accuracy of their reports; that facts are important; that reporters should be editorially independent of advertisers and other groups.

To properly asses the model we need to delve deeply into its conceptual scheme. The problem was the model's conception of *how* journalists were to report factually, accurately, and with a minimum of bias. The model prescribed a narrow and demanding form of objective reporting that was implausible – a neutrality that allowed no community engagement; reports that allegedly expressed no perspective, no value judgments; and a reporting of events that was "just the facts," a pure, factual description somehow stripped of all interpretation.

Conclusion

The overall aim of this book is to persuade – and provoke – ethicists, journalists, students, and members of the public to disrupt and invent.

Chapter 2 disrupts (and overcomes) the dualisms of the traditional model by proposing a holistic mindset. Chapter 3 disrupts the belief in detachment or a strict neutrality, and proposes a theory of engaged journalism. Chapter 4 disrupts patriotism as the "master norm" of parochial journalism ethics, and proposes a global approach to the field. Chapter 5 examines how journalists, in collaboration with others, can help to detox a polluted public sphere, and resist fake news and extreme populism. With Chapter 6, the book concludes with my imagining the shape of a future journalism ethics, employing notions proposed throughout the book.

Notes

1 Dworkin, *Law's Empire*, 52.
2 On ideologies as systems of ideas that endow meaning, see Freeden, *Ideology*.
3 See Kuhn, *The Structure of Scientific Revolutions*.
4 See Ward, *Ethics and the Media*, 59–61.
5 On similarities and differences about values among journalists worldwide, see the *Worlds of Journalism* project www.worldsofjournalism.org/. For a list of codes of ethics, see http://ethicnet.uta.fi/codes_by_country.
6 For details on the emergence of the professional objective model, see my *The Invention of Journalism Ethics*.
7 The model has influenced the construction of journalism codes of ethics in non-Western countries. For example, in 2017, I was consultant to a media research center in Vietnam which developed an ethical code for the nation's press. The code incorporated principles of the professional objective model.
8 See Ward, "Journalism Ethics in a Digital Era."
9 See Baldasty, *The Commercialization of the News in the Nineteenth Century*, and Campbell, *Yellow Journalism*.
10 Schudson, *Discovering the News*, and Mindich, *Just the Facts*.

2   Disrupt dualisms – holism

The first step in disrupting journalism ethics is to disrupt the professional objective model, and to propose an alternative model. I do so in this chapter. I reject two central notions of the model: neutrality and an objectivity of "just the facts." I replace them with the idea of objective engagement. I do not reject objectivity tout court. I reject a flawed, dualistic understanding of objectivity as neutral fact-stating. I propose a better conception, holistic or pragmatic objectivity.

For the professional model, neutrality and what I call the "objectivity of hard facts" are the core concepts of its moral interpretation of journalism. The good reporter is as neutral and fact-based as a court stenographer when she reports on comments and actions in a trial. Non-neutral approaches to reporting, such as interpretive and advocacy journalism, violate journalism ethics because they allow personal bias and subjective interests to distort reports. The point of journalism is to inform the public by chronicling events from the stance of a *neutral stenographer of just the hard facts*. The moral interpretation leads to the endorsement of more specific norms and practices, such as the direct quotation of sources and the careful attribution and balancing of opinion in stories.

Section 1: dueling dualisms

The moral interpretation is expressed in dualistic terms.

To employ a dualism is to explain something in terms of two completely different things.[1] For example, Descartes's famous mind-body dualism regards humans as composed of two completely different substances, mind and matter. Dualists draw hard lines between pairs of things, such as life and death, ying and yang, heaven and hell, saints and sinners, desire and rationality. Some dualisms are "antagonistic." That is, the components are thought to be antagonistic to each other. So, it is good versus evil, desire versus reason, egoism versus altruism, or truth versus falsehood. Frequently, dualisms are criticized as simplistic views of complex phenomena. Ethics, it is opined, contains problems where things are not "black or white." Yet, for all we know, some dualisms may be correct. So we need an argument as to why particular dualisms are incorrect.

Neutrality and facts

In the objective model, two dualisms explain the difference between good and bad practice: the dualism of *neutrality versus engagement*, and the duality of *fact versus interpretation*. As a stance, neutrality is completely different from, and often antagonistic to, engagement; and facts (or factual statements) are completely different from, and often antagonistic, to interpretations (or interpretive statements). The responsible reporter guides her practice by honoring the terms on the left-hand side of both dualisms, neutrality and factuality, while avoiding what falls under the right-hand side, engagement and interpretation.

It is important to note two things: (1) the notions of neutrality and objectivity of fact are specific understandings of detachment and objectivity. There are other understandings. For instance, there are notions of objectivity that do not reduce it to knowing only hard facts. (2) Neutrality and objectivity are philosophical notions with a long history. They are part of Western culture's centuries-old effort to say what constitutes objective knowledge and how it is obtained. When journalists endorse neutrality and objectivity they adopt, knowingly or unknowingly, a particular view of the mind and how it knows the world. They commit themselves to an epistemology – a view of knowledge and good inquiry. In the case of the model, it is a late form of empiricism where the neutral apprehension of facts separates fact from fiction, the objective from the subjective.

Therefore, the validity of the model rests on the validity of the dualisms, and their epistemology. To judge the validity of the dualisms requires more than checking how they work in journalism practice. It requires a philosophical critique of their epistemology, i.e., the plausibility of its psychological and methodological premises, and an awareness of how these dualisms have been critiqued in the past. As I have said, these premises are implausible, and, by the turn of the 20th century, philosophers, scientists, and other thinkers were abandoning this dualistic understanding of objectivity and knowledge.[2]

Before I say why the dualisms are implausible, I need to explain in more detail the understandings of neutral and objectivity in question, and how they form dualisms.

The model's emphasis on neutrality is strong and emphatic. Responsible reporters should be completely neutral when reporting on society.

Neutrality is about the psychological stance that a virtuous reporter adopts in the reporting process. Reporters exhibit neutrality by not showing favoritism to any group or viewpoint, e.g., by inserting their own evaluations and perspectives into the story. Neutrality requires detachment from what they report on, i.e., reporters do not participate in politics or advocacy. Neutrality requires disengagement, i.e., reporters do not use their reporting to realize personal or social goals.

Neutrality encourages the view that journalists are spectators (or detached viewers) of the world, reporting what happens around them, and what other people do and say. Journalists report what rival groups do in the public sphere, and what they say about policies, but, in their reports, they do not judge which group is right or wrong. They include opinions in reports but they are the opinions of other people. They treat an opinion as a fact – the fact that someone expressed an opinion. Journalists report on advocates and social movements, but they do not advocate or join movements. They do not help candidates get elected during campaigns. Journalists report on partisans but are not themselves partisan. As good stenographers, reporters faithfully record and transmit what happens in the public sphere, then they let citizens judge for themselves. This portrait of the neutral journalist is set over and against the journalist who is engaged socially.

Objectivity of hard facts does not focus, like neutrality, on the psychological attitude of reporters. It is a norm concerned with *what* is reported, with the content of reports. The main content of reports should be facts – facts about what happened, facts about who said what. But not just any sort of fact. In philosophy, facts are liberally identified with whatever is true – where truth is a correspondence of belief to the way the world really is. A fact is any true assertion, empirical, theoretical, or mathematical, about any state of affairs or object in the world; and, vice versa, a truth is a fact. Grass is green is true if it is a fact that grass is green. Darwin's theory of natural selection is a fact if it is a true theory of evolution.

But, in journalism, "fact" typically refers to a narrower range of statements: empirical, non-theoretical, statements that describe observations of events and actors. Journalistic facts are (1) truths we know based on our empirical experiences, and (2) beliefs reached by careful generalization upon empirical experiences, such as factual studies by experts, numerical analysis of data, or facts established by science.

Why are facts hard?

Why are these facts called "hard"? For two reasons. First, a fact of experience is hard because it exists independently of human thinking and goals. They just *are*. Period. With facts we stub our toe on the real world. Facts are not what we wish were true but what is true. This hard, independent world of facts, external to our mind, decides whether a statement is true or false, objective or subjective. Facts are hard nuggets of unimpeachable data about the world that all rational people must recognize. Second, facts are hard because they resist the influence of human psychology – our wishes, desires, interests, and theories. Facts are not the product of our thinking and emotions. Water is H_2O no matter what anyone thinks about it.

Interpretations, by contrast, seek to bestow meaning on the world of facts – what facts mean, imply or portend. Meanings are soft, mental constructions, not hard facts. Interpretations include theories, hypotheses, conjectures, speculations, predictions, and value judgments. Interpretations are fallible, and are presumed to be true relative to our conceptual schemes and beliefs. Also, they are plural: reasonable people can hold different interpretations of the same set of facts, just as there exist rival scientific theories even after all available facts are known. Hard facts are interpretation-neutral, theory-neutral, and value-neutral. As neutral data, facts can serve as impartial adjudicators of interpretations.

This view leads to a skeptical view of what human psychology contributes to inquiry into truth or the real world. Medieval philosophers claimed that men could not know the world on their own because they were corrupted by a sinful body. Modern objectivists of hard facts endorse a secular version of this claim. Humans need stern, methodological restraints on inquiry because we are corrupted by biased faculties, such as our emotions. Given the biasing power of emotion or self-interest, it seems that one should seek truth by restricting oneself to the collection of facts, and then grounding whatever else we say *on* those facts in a rigorous manner. Theory must be viewed with suspicion, constantly checked, and, like a large balloon, tied down to earth by facts. Otherwise, it will fly off to a world of abstraction and metaphysical fantasy in the clouds. In epistemology, one should privilege the "hard" faculties of observation, logic, numbers, and mathematical reasoning. At the same time, one should repress the soft, psychological faculties of valuing, emotion, and passion, especially where such faculties are put to work by rhetorical argument, value-laden reasoning, social engagement, and advocacy.

This dualism is the philosophical "picture" of objective knowledge to which the professional model is committed. If you press on the model's epistemology hard enough, it must fall back on the idea of hard facts and soft interpretations. The picture is historically significant. It is a view of inquiry that follows from the 17th-century epistemology of scientific empiricism, virtually created by Francis Bacon with his stress on a new method to "scrub clean" our judgments until we reach pure facts.[3] Three centuries later, in the early 1900s, the logical positivists, one of the most influential movements in modern philosophy, sought to reduce all meaningful and scientific statements to statements of pure, non-interpreted observations or experiences. Scientific knowledge had to be constructed from pure, hard facts.[4] It was this epistemology of hard facts, combined with an ascendant professionalism that stressed objectivity, which influenced the journalists who created the model.

Stern empiricism

What is distinct about this ideology of neutral factuality in its application to journalism? What is distinct is not that the ideology talks about facts and asks journalists to watch their biases. It makes good sense – and has been said since the dawn of modern journalism – that journalists should be careful with facts. It makes good sense – and this also has been said since the dawn of modern journalism – that journalists should seek some degree of impartiality.[5] What is unique about the model is its stern empiricism, its dualistic conceptions of neutrality and factuality, and the non-compromising newsroom rules for constructing stories.

In the late 1800s, journalism's increased attention to reporting news encouraged an informal, robust empiricism that sent reporters out into the world to chronicle events. But this empiricism allowed for interpretation, opinion, and sensational accounts or "color" by reporters. By the early 1900s, there was decreasing tolerance for such departures from reporting the facts. The professional objective model codified this trend. It was a strict, methodological empiricism that required reporters to follow a host of rules to eliminate any lurking interpretation in reports. The capital sin of a reporter, as so many editors and books on reporting said, was to "editorialize" in one's news report. To "editorialize" was to express an opinion or evaluation. The method did not call for trying to reduce one's opinions or interpretations; it called for the *elimination* of the reporter's opinions and interpretations. Also, the method did not call on reporters to try to reduce their partialities – or to be transparent about them. It called on reporters to *eliminate* or repress such attachments. The objective model was a policing action against engagement and interpretation in reporting.

Key presuppositions: a summary

To critique the model, we need to bear in mind its key philosophical presuppositions.

• *the inquirer as spectator, not engaged agent:* The objective model portrays the reporter as a spectator on their times, and their society.

Reporters observe events, take notes, quote leaders, and record events from a neutral distance. The Pythagoreans of Ancient Greece viewed philosophy as objective observations of the world going on around the philosopher. Lovers of knowledge were "detached observers of men's lesser games."[6] Reporters should be the Pythagoreans of the public sphere. Pragmatist John Dewey, one of the greatest anti-dualism philosophers, called this the "spectator conception of knowledge."[7]

- *neutrality, not impartiality:* The model adopts neutrality as the stance of the good reporter. Neutrality is a strong psychological requirement, incompatible with engagement.

- *encapsulation of observation of fact:* Objectivity of hard facts presumes that humans (and journalists) have a stand-alone or independent capacity to know facts, apart from their capacity to interpret, to seek goals, and to value. The faculties that allow us to interpret things and assign meanings must be kept separate from the capacity to know facts. The faculty of observing (or knowing) must be *encapsulated*, operating independently of the influence of biasing psychological capacities.

- *direct contact with world:* Objectivity of hard facts presumes that people, mainly through observation, have direct awareness of the world as it is. Knowledge of fact is knowledge of reality as it exists apart from human conceptualization and interests. Knowledge of hard facts is unmediated by conceptual schemes and other soft, mental representations.

- *neutral objectivity of hard facts is one-dimensional and reductionist:* Objectivity of hard facts reduces objectivity to one dimension: verification of claims by information from one dimension of experience, observation of facts of the world.

Section 2: an alternative – pragmatic holism

If this dualistic epistemology of journalism is flawed, if its key presuppositions are questionable, then the question is: what is the alternative? How else can we think about good inquiry, truth, and objectivity in journalism? It is time for me to spell out my alternative, which I call pragmatic holism or pragmatic objectivity.

My alternative is a thorough-going holism of experience and of inquiry. It undercuts dualisms while reformulating impartiality and objectivity so they are more defensible theoretically and more applicable to today's journalism. My philosophy of journalism is grounded in the ideas of tested interpretation and engagement for democracy.

A full presentation of the philosophy is beyond this book. It would take us into philosophical, psychological, and ethical theory. However, in the rest of this chapter, I provide an overview of pragmatic holism. In the rest of the book, I spell out how pragmatic holism changes how we think about journalism ethics.

Agency as primary

Pragmatic holism is pragmatic because it is designed to guide practical professions such as journalism. Also, it is pragmatic in its starting point, conceptually. It starts with, and makes primary, the human as agent, as actor-in-the-world. Agents employ their psychological capacities – to conceive, plan, and evaluate – to pursue personal and social purposes. The agent always has purposes, even when seeking to be impartial. All thinking, even scientific or philosophical thinking, is embedded within praxis, within activities we consider valuable. Also, the agent is situated. She engages the world within a social context in a time and place. She is inculcated into a culture of ideas, values, problems, and ways of practice. In seeking goals, the agent finds in her environment both resources and obstacles. She inherits traditions that should be defended and traditions to be overcome.

Pragmatic holism does not start with, nor does it make primary, the inquirer regarded as a spectator. When humans become spectators, they restrain their robust agency. For whatever reasons, they prefer to be disengaged from the events that swirl around him, observing and commenting on the passing show of life, or some part of life. They maintain a distance from the passionate, purpose-led agents acting and competing in the public sphere.

Becoming a spectator is one form of being in the world that agents can adopt. It is also a stance that journalists can adopt.[8] But pragmatic holism thinks that humans are first and foremost engaged agents, especially in professions such as journalism. Even when we are neutral objectivists of fact, we are operating, covertly, as agents, acting according to unstated values and purposes. In life, there is no value-free zone, no relief from the burdens of agency.

Holism of experience

Pragmatic holism contends that the experience of agents, the way these agents inquire into the world and the way they evaluate their findings, is a holistic process. Therefore, we should adopt a holistic perspective in inquiry.

What is this perspective? Rather than attempting to understand things by dividing them into dualisms, i.e., two separate components, holism explains things as the interaction of many components. The components entangle, converge, and work together. They form a system. The elements are entangled the way that the different strains in a rope are intertwined, or the way nodes are connected to form a web. We cannot adequately understand individual components apart from the system in which it occurs. The part is known through the whole, as the meaning of a word is known through the language in which it occurs.

This is an abstract depiction of holism. To be more concrete, apply this approach to our everyday experiences. Holism regards our experience of the world as the result of an inseparable and irreducible mix of psychological and bodily capacities. Take, for example, my experience now as I write this book; your interpretation of a poem; our experience of watching Hamlet on stage; the concert violinist's activity as she performs a complex sonata with an orchestra; or a scientist seeking to understand a phenomena or test a theory. These experiences result from the convergence and entanglement of capacities such as observation, reasoning, feeling, imagining, conjecturing, unconscious information processing, body memory, valuing, and goal-seeking. These components are inseparable in reality. One can, for purposes of analysis, concentrate on a particular component, such as how our eyes track moving objects, or study the interaction of two capacities, such as the role of memory in perception. But a holist never forgets that these activities are part of a much thicker experience. For the holist, "experience" is rich and wide, not parsimonious and narrow. It is this wide experience that justifies claims.

Holism opposes an atomistic approach which isolates one capacity and makes it a privileged faculty and source of justified belief. This is what the dualisms above attempt to do. They separate out one capacity, such as observation of external objects (or facts). They postulate that it operates, in encapsulated form, apart from the wide experiences of humans. This narrow slice of our experience is supposed to justify all else.

Unfortunately, for the atomist, there is no "atomistic" reduction of experience to one privileged capacity. There is no encapsulated faculty for grasping facts. And, no separate, unmediated, contact with reality. Even ordinary perceptions and beliefs are shot through with our concepts, expectations, norms, presumptions, prior knowledge, memory, and interests. This does not mean that perception and empirical facts play no role in experience or in inquiry. They do, and they do so in important ways. It means that the value of perception and empirical facts resides in their contribution to our wide experiences, and our evaluation of those experiences. For example, empirical experiments may question a theoretical belief, or new facts can challenge our goals.

Holism of experience entails that interpretation, not observation of hard facts is our primary mode of knowing the world. Interpretation is inherently holistic. It bestows meaning on our experiences by using a plurality of capacities, from our memory of past experience to our ability to conceptualize a new work of art. Since our beliefs and narratives emerge from this rich experience, holism contends that all beliefs and narratives are interpretations. There is no reporting just the facts, apart from everything else, in any walk of life. No narrative purely describes the world as it is, apart from human cognition, perspective, and interpretation. Facts are those interpretations that we consider evidently true. As Putnam stressed, what we regard as a fact depends on norms, i.e., facts are those beliefs that satisfy norms of rationality, logic, and coherence with other facts. Facts depend on norms. The fact-value dichotomy is a myth.[9] Data only makes sense relative to a larger framework of concepts and meanings. Without such contextualization, data would not be data for us, as agents.

There is perhaps no more succinct debunking of the idea that isolated facts have a special power by themselves than John Dewey's introduction to *The Public and Its Problems*.[10] In a few pages, Dewey throws cold water on the idea that facts "carry their meaning along on themselves on their face." There may be disagreement on the facts or on what they mean. There may be insufficient facts to establish a claim. The same facts may support rival interpretations. Purported facts may be false or manipulated. Dewey points out that a few recalcitrant facts need never force a person to accept or abandon a particular theory about what the facts mean. After Dewey, Quine argued that holism shows that facts never "prove" an empirical theory. There is always the possibility of an equally good, rival theory. Just as facts "under-determine" scientific theory, so they under-determine our news reports.[11]

We are, and must be to survive, constant interpreters. We use conceptual schemes to grasp an object, to explain it. We interpret smoke on the horizon as a ship at sea. We interpret a comment as sarcastic. We interpret light as quanta of energy. We interpret Hamlet as both mad and cunning as he plots to revenge his father's death. We interpret that yellow extra-terrestrial body as the morning sun, a ball of inflamed gasses that the earth encircles. These "facts" are interpretations that result from the application of conceptual schemes, not the bald observation of the sun as a perceptual sensation or the bare perception of Hamlet striding across the stage.[12]

Interpretations are holistic creatures. There is no digging down below interpretation to a more basic realm of non-interpreted data, some pre-interpretive facts, or what empiricists call the "given" in experience. Non-interpreted data must be interpreted before they play any role in our cognitive economy. As reporters, we interpret data in the same holistic manner. We interpret the out-going police chief's faint praise for his replacement as limited support for his successor. We interpret the American president's threat to withdraw the broadcasting license of a news organization as a violation of the country's First Amendment.

Objective inquiry, holistically defined, is the organized, critical, and self-conscious, attempt to reach insightful, defensible *interpretations* of whatever is the focus of study or practice. Inquiry is not about limiting oneself to illusory pure facts or unmediated contact with the world. It is not about eliminating interpretation to arrive at facts scrubbed clean.

Pragmatic or holistic objectivity[13]

If interpretations are "soft," how do we know when an interpretation is correct, or better than others? What does holism say about the epistemic evaluation of beliefs?

Staying true to agency-based holism, we begin by viewing evaluation as another part of our agency, our wide experience, and our penchant to interpret experiences. Objective evaluation is the *evaluation of holistic experiences by holistic means*, or holistic objectivity.

We evaluate interpretations by using some framework of evaluation – a set of evaluative criteria. The inquirer adopts the objective stance, the attitude of a person willing to step back from their beliefs, to follow the facts where they lead, and so on. Then the agent evaluates interpretations using criteria from two levels: (1) a general set of criteria that defines what it is for any inquirer to be rational. We seek to make our interpretations logically consistent, coherent with other knowledge, clear in concept and definition, and based on empirical support. Any interpretation must satisfy these criteria to some tolerable extent to be a candidate for objective knowledge. (2) An additional set of criteria that says what being rational means in particular practices. For example, health scientists not only abide by the general norm of logical consistency, they also have tests for evaluating activities specific to their practice, such as evaluating clinical trials for new drugs. Their objective criteria for clinical trials include taking into account the null hypothesis, and whether the trial was double or triple blind. Similarly, pollsters have a range of criteria for evaluating polls, such as the size and randomness of the sample. Journalists have specific norms and protocols for evaluating stories, from checking the reliability of a source to having at least two independent sources on a major investigative story.

This evaluation is holistic. Inquirers balance and weigh a variety of norms to determine to what degree an interpretation is likely to be true, accurate, and objective. Inquirers do not check only one type of criteria, e.g., if the interpretation fits the available facts of observation. This is the atomistic approach of objectivity of hard facts. Instead, holists ask if, for example, a new hypothesis is consistent with existing theory, if the methodology was rigorous and designed to avoid bias, and so on. Not only is our interpretation of experience holistic but our evaluation of the interpretation is *also* holistic.

Therefore, we arrive at a notion of objectivity for situated, agency-driven inquiry: objectivity is the holistic testing of interpretations according to the best available evaluative criteria, both general and practice-specific. These norms of evaluation are not absolute but historical. They are the norms that in the past have served inquiry well in certain cultures and eras. They evolve.

I call pragmatic objectivity "objectivity with a human face" because it does not seek an absolute (or certain) judgment about the objectivity of inter-pretations. Rather, it is the imperfect, all-too-human task of critiquing beliefs that are tied closely to purposes and situations. The judgment of objectivity is relative and a matter of degree: interpretation x is more objective than interpretation y relative to our evaluative criteria. Yet, because of its human face, holistic objectivity is a better model of what actually happens in inquiry and, because of its pragmatism, a more useful guide for social practices like journalism. Absolutists about knowledge might complain that an objectivity that is relative to humans and their purposes is not really objectivity at all. It is not enough. How do we *really* know whether our interpretations map reality? But what does *really* mean? As agents we cannot get outside of our minds and see if our ideas correspond to the world as it is, apart from human conceptualization. We know reality only through the mediation of imperfect methods of situated agents. Objectivity with a human face *better* be enough, since it is the only objectivity we will ever have.

Section 3: engagement and objectivity

Approaching inquiry and objectivity from the view of a pragmatic, agent-centered philosophy is an important step but it does not answer all ques-tions. I want to reply to questions that I presume are lurking in the reader's mind, such as how one can be engaged and objective at the same time, what is the difference between being neutral and being impartial, and what is the role of emotions? To some people, my idea of objective interpretation seems contradictory, given the legacy of our cultural dualisms.

Engagement: agency in society

The etymology of "engagement" revolves around three senses: being occu-pied with something; finding something interesting or entertaining; and being committed.

We are occupied when we perform a role or job. Teachers are engaged in classrooms. Being occupied also means being engrossed by some activ-ity, e.g., learning to paint watercolors. We are engaged with something as entertaining when something grabs our attention, such as when we say it was an engaging play. Engagement is commitment when we undertake some serious course of action, or pursue some complex, difficult-to-reach goal. One gets "involved" with someone or some process where withdrawal is difficult, e.g., to engage in combat, to get married, to devote one's life to helping street people. What these senses have in common is intentional human agency.

The opposite of engagement is disengagement, which can take two forms – global or local. Global disengagement is an overall withdrawal from agency, often caused by a decline in interest in the world. One may take little interest in the plans of others, or in the issues that roil social life. One can withdraw to one's study, become an ironic spectator, or a hermit. Local disengagement means that a person is not engaged in *this* issue, or *that* activity, or *these* groups, at *this* time.

In this book, engagement means being an agent who is committed. Engagement involves a significant amount of activity, bodily agency, pursuit of goals, and adherence to practices. We can be engaged with theoretical problems and intellectual activities. However, this type of engagement is not the focus of this chapter. Engagement in this book refers primarily to social engagement. People are engaged to maintain certain forms of community, including acting to reform society and its political structure. Engaged activity includes performing an important social practice, protesting government policy, being an activist for a new law, or acting as an official who, for example, protects the environment from corporate polluters. Depending on the cause, the people engaged, and the methods employed, engagement can have a positive or negative meaning for the public. We have names for some of these engaged people. We call some of them partisans or ideologues; some we call advocates; some we call activists. I do not restrict "engaged citizen" to the familiar stereotypes of the protesting activist or strong partisan. Judges, too, can be "activists" in changing outdated laws. Journalists can be advocates.

How, then, is holistic objectivity compatible with being engaged? They are compatible in the same way that means and ends, or methods and goals, are different but compatible.

Engagement is about goals. Objectivity is about means and methods. Objectivity is a means to certain goals, such as truthful interpretations and unbiased decisions. Objectivity is a method that requires interpreters to adopt a certain stance and honor rational norms of evaluation. Objectivity and engagement are compatible because they are different aspects of agency. I am partial about my goals. I prefer certain goals over others. Yet, at the same time, I can be impartial in how I seek the goals. Scientists follow objective methods to explain phenomena and create new technology. Judges follow the objective methods of law to pursue justice. The value of objectivity is that it helps us to be intelligently and fairly engaged.

Impartiality, not neutrality

Neutrality is not the correct term for describing the stance of purposeful agents who seek objective judgments. Impartiality is the correct term.

"Neutrality" derives from the idea that something belongs to neither of two things, or two opposites. Originally, neutrality's meaning was sexual, i.e., to be neuter – neither masculine nor feminine. In chemistry, a neutral solution is neither acidic nor basic. In physics, a neutral particle is without electrical charge. When applied in social contexts, neutrality means that, when a dispute arises, we do not take sides, the way a country can be neutral in a war between other nations. One does not assist one of the sides in any manner. To be neutral is to be detached. My car is in "neutral" when the driveshaft is not attached to any gear that moves the vehicle.

The correct stance for engaged inquiry is impartiality, defined as not allowing partialities to unduly influence and distort judgment. Genuine inquiry derives from an impartial search for the truth, "regardless of what the color of that truth may be."[14] "Undue" means the partiality leads you to judge selfishly or subjectively. The partiality distorts the accuracy, truthfulness, or fairness of your thinking. Bias is a persistent disposition to favor certain beliefs or conduct, regardless of the evidence. The term "bias" originally referred to a bowling ball that would consistently roll to the left or right, regardless of the terrain or the way it was thrown. Similarly, our partialities can persistently lead us to affirm unfair or badly evidenced judgments. With impartiality, agents acknowledge their partialities. Yet partialities are not viewed as necessarily distorting. Partialities can be good or bad; they give us goals and endow meaning on activity. The point of talking about impartiality is not to eliminate partialities, which is impossible in any case. It is to (a) raise to awareness the existence of one's partialities in a situation and to be transparent about them to oneself and others; and (b) to be sensitive to the undue influence of these partialities.

One way to monitor partialities is to apply the criteria of pragmatic objectivity: to ask whether your judgment is ignoring inconvenient facts, is not coherent with other beliefs, and so on. You apply the rational standards to oneself. Another way is to submit your thinking to others. Objectivity is best applied in groups. Are you willing to submit your thinking to public scrutiny? Are the reasons you give the sorts of reasons that other, reasonable people would accept as valid? How does your perspective mesh with the perspectives of others? In the end, holistic objectivity is intersubjective objectivity. To be objective, parties to any discussion should adopt what Sen has called an attitude of "open impartiality" which is an openness to arguments from others and their perspectives and interests.[15] If your thinking fails these standards, you have reason to believe that a partiality is unduly affecting you.

Impartiality is a stance for responsibly engaged people – professors, referees, journalists, and others. Impartiality does not mean that one has no feelings, or no views on some matter. It does not mean that one does not feel the tug of one's own biases and interests. It does not mean one must withdraw from agency, detached like the neutral gear in my car. It does not require that one can never express a judgment, conclusion, or perspective. What impartiality demands is that agents partially transcend their partialities but never repress them entirely.

Consider some examples of impartiality-in-action. Take the case of an impartial judge adjudicating a dispute. The judge does eventually "take" sides, i.e., she eventually judges that one side in a dispute has the better case in law. The judge judges. She draws conclusions. She interprets. Impartial judging means that the judge adopts the objective stance by not prejudging the case, and applies the generic standards of rationality and the domain-specific standards of the law. Or, consider the Red Cross, which is famous for its neutrality among warring sides. I think the Red Cross's neutrality is misnamed. What they practice is impartiality-in-action. The Red Cross is far from being detached from or uninterested in the wars in which it intervenes. The Red Cross acts. It has goals. It enters war zones to help injured combatants and distressed citizens. But it tries to not let the partialities of staff (or its organization) bias their treatment of any side in the dispute. Similarly, impartial UN officials may be asked to investigate whether a military leader violated human rights. Or, a team of investigative journalists, after extensive impartial investigation into the facts of a case, may conclude that an official acted wrongly, and against the public interest. Impartiality is crucial for fair engagement, and should not be confused with a spineless avoidance of taking a stand.

Rational passions

A crude but widespread belief among the legion of critics of objectivity is that impartiality and objectivity are neither possible nor desirable because they require agents to turn themselves into cold-blooded spectators on the urgent issues of life.

But why should this be so? Why set impartiality and objectivity against the passions and emotions – those central motivators of human conduct? Why think objectivity is impossible?

Throughout history, the greatest inquirers, artists, journalists, and scientists have exhibited a passionate commitment to impartiality: Plato's impassioned attempts to design a "rational" republic resistant to demagogues; Einstein's passion to discover the truths of relativity theory; Woodward and Bernstein's passionate search for facts to reveal corruption and criminality in the Nixon White House. Humans are perhaps the only creatures that have rational passions, or passions that seek rational and ethical goals. Humans exhibit a passion to know and learn, a determination to solve riddles, and a passion for fairness. Humans also have cognitive emotions – such as wonder, curiosity, and awe.[16] Therefore, there is no contradiction in stating that objectivity is a passionate commitment to impartial inquiry. Impartiality means caring so much for the honest truth that one does not allow personal interests to subvert inquiry or to prejudge the issue. When impartial people see bias and partiality twisting the public's understanding of some matter, or badly influencing conduct, they experience frustration, even anger. Objectivity is a rational passion for objective knowledge and disinterested decisions.

This link between inquiry, passion, and impartiality is typically not emphasized because of the way our culture portrays rationality and objectivity. Perhaps the classic portrait of the "rational" person is Thomas Gradgrind, the cold-blooded school board superintendent in Charles Dicken's novel, *Hard Times*, who treats all questions, including interactions with his children, in terms of numbers, facts, and expected utility. Critics of objectivity then ask rhetorically: who would support an attitude like that? The correct response is no one should. Impartiality and objectivity do not require people to become a "logic machine" – a Dr. Spock.[17] In ethics, appeals to compassion and empathy should be part of rational arguments about ethical decisions. Moreover, the best practices of objectivity combine partiality and impartiality. In a criminal trial, the partialities of the prosecutor and the defense attorney (and the parties they represent) occur within a larger impartial context – evaluation by a judge or jury. The latter subjects partial arguments to the test of objective evidence and impartial rules of law. Ideally, what is fair and objective emerges from a sort of "trial by fire" – a trial where partial arguments are tested.

Why do we think that objectivity is too much to ask of people? Again, we can look to our culture. In Ancient Greece, Parmenides argued that he found the true path to absolute knowledge by transcending human affairs and using only his reason. Plato, despite his passionate rationality, makes the search for objective knowledge a special and difficult ascent to the intellectual grasp of eternal verities – a path available only to the most rational and wisest of men. From Plato to Descartes and beyond, Western thinking on knowledge has portrayed objectivity and knowledge as requiring a grasp of absolute truth. Objectivity requires almost super-human effort and a setting aside of engagement in human affairs.

This perspective forgets the humble beginnings of objectivity in our need to evaluate everyday beliefs through an impartial process that is imperfect, yet within the reach of many people. It takes no Parmenides to apply the criteria of holistic objectivity. It takes discipline, yes, but not super-human perfection. Too much time has been spent of late on the flabby, vague question of whether objectivity exists. Of course it exists, if by "exists" we mean that it is a method of evaluation that many people can apply. People can be objective, in this sense, to a significant degree. In fact, people adopt the objective stance every day: students expect their teachers to give them a fair grade on a test based on objective criteria; defendants in court expect the judge to be objective; committees that choose scholarships, or awards for great journalism, work very hard to refine and apply objective criteria. What would students, defendants, and applicants for awards say if their teachers, judges, and committees simply said: "Well, as you know, academics have proved there is no such thing as objectivity, so we won't try to exemplify what does not exist. So we will judge you in any way we feel like!" The students, defendants, and applicants would cry out for objectivity, for impartiality. This scenario may seem surreal. But it is not far from the way objectivity is treated in society. People are quite sure, intellectually, there is no such thing as objectivity until they need it in practice. The public is sure there is no such thing as objectivity yet they complain that the news media is not objective. Our culture is, to say the least, conflicted on this matter.

Much of the criticism of impartiality and objectivity is a caricature of how we actually evaluate beliefs in everyday life. It is a "straw man" argument that attacks a position – perfect objectivity – not held by reasonable proponents of objectivity. Objectivity with a human face does not require perfect objectivity. It requires only that a person is capable, *to some significant or satisfactory degree*, to discipline their partialities. Shallow critics of objectivity never tire of saying: "We all have biases." They think this disproves objectivity yet it actually proves why we need objectivity. The norms of objectivity were not constructed because its creators thought most humans were "empty" of bias. The norms were constructed *because* of an acute awareness of bias. We biased humans need the discipline of objectivity to *reduce* the influence of bias where it threatens judgment.

Emotions as cognitive

Another reason for either denying objectivity or reducing objectivity to hard facts is that our culture works with a pinched understanding of the emotions.

Like the dualism of fact and interpretation, people erect an antagonistic dualism of emotion and cognition. Emotions are viewed as non-cognitive in nature and a threat to correct cognition. "Cognition" refers to psychological capacities, e.g. perception or conceptualization, which help us to apprehend objects in the world. To call emotions "non-cognitive" is to say they have literally nothing (or very little) to do with our understanding of the world. A popular view is that emotions are non-rational. They are impulses that cause us to have certain feelings and to do certain things. These impulses can only be channeled and controlled, not "reasoned with" since they have no cognitive element. Emotions, it is concluded, are enemies of the objective stance.

Fortunately, recent work in the theory of emotion has challenged this dualism. Martha Nussbaum, for example, promotes a "cognitive-evaluative" notion of emotion.[18] Nussbaum starts with our common sense list of emotions – grief, fear, hatred, love, anger, envy, jealousy, and empathy. She distinguishes them from desires, "objectless" moods like feeling irritable, bodily states such as hunger and thirst, and bodily sensations such as shivering when afraid. Nussbaum then adopts a neo-Stoic "cognitive" (or a "cognitive-evaluative") view of the emotions. It views the emotions as "intelligent" not because they always guide us rationally and wisely, but because they have an important cognitive element. She rejects the idea that emotions are unthinking energies that "simply push people around" and whose presumed opposition to rationality means they should be excluded from ethical deliberation.

Nussbaum regards emotions as "intelligent responses to the perception of value." The cognitive content of emotions consists in how we understand and evaluate the object. All emotions involve an (a) intentional thought or perception directed at an object and (b) some type of evaluative appraisal of the importance or salience of objects. Emotional responses are judgments about an object; these emotional judgments are a subclass of value judgments.[19] "Emotions," she writes, "view the world from the point of view of my own scheme of goals and projects, the things to which I attach value in a conception of what it is for me to live well."[20]

The entanglement of emotion and belief is clear when we consider how the difference between fearing and loving a person depends on cognition. It depends on our beliefs about the person, and information about the world. Moreover, our deepest emotions are entangled with our beliefs and goals. For example, the visceral pain of grieving a spouse "violently tears the fabric of attachment, hope, and expectation that we have built around that person."[21] That fabric is comprised of beliefs, goals, interpretations, and other cognitive elements. Also, our emotional response to a piece of music involves a cognitive interpretation of the lyrics and musical phrases. Moreover, emotions are shaped by social norms and specific circumstances. Even biologically "given" emotions such as anger are expressed in different ways in different societies. Our emotional response to artistic productions, e.g., watching Shylock ask for his "pound of flesh" in Shakespeare's *The Merchant of Venice*, is mediated by our norms, knowledge of history, and ways of interpreting the play.

Philosopher Nelson Goodman has provided further arguments, drawn from art, for considering emotions as much more than brute feelings, and part of our cognitive understanding of the world. In *Languages of Art*, Goodman stresses the cognitive function of emotion in art. Goodman starts his analysis as I have done: decrying the "domineering dichotomy" between the cognitive and the emotive. In this view, science is cognitive but art, and our responses to it, are matters of emotion that tells us much about our psychological profile but little that is objective about the work of art. Goodman complains that this dichotomy keeps us from seeing that, in aesthetic experience, "the *emotions function cognitively*."[22] Emotional "numbness," he says, disables us as completely as blindness or deafness. Emotions provide access to, and call our attention to, aspects of objects, such as works of art, that we might otherwise not notice or appreciate. Emotion in aesthetic experience "is a means of discerning what properties a work has and expresses." The cognitive use of emotions in art involves discriminating and relating felt emotions so as to grasp the work "and integrate it with the rest of our experience and the world."[23] Aesthetic experience is dynamic, not static. It includes making subtle discriminations and discerning subtle relationships, identifying symbolic systems and what characters within these systems denote or exemplify.

Using my terms, the experience of a work of art is a holistic interaction between emotions, facts, the environment, perceived qualities such as colors, and the more abstract apprehension of how elements in the work of art are ordered. We have a wide experience.

Therefore, we must be careful *not* to exclude emotions from our theory of how we objectively apprehend the world around us, whether it is science, journalism, or art. However, this does not mean that we do not need to be critically attentive to the emotions we have and how we use them. We need to know when certain types of emotion (and certain degrees of emotions) are appropriate or inappropriate, and what sorts of emotions are conducive or not conducive to achieving personal and communal goals. Our capacity to have emotions, like our capacity to observe, to imagine, and to reason, need to be used wisely. As Aristotle thought, our emotions and our virtues are matters of habit and education. So it *is* true that emotions can lead us astray. We can overact to events; we can be filled with anger or hatred; our emotional attachments can blind us to objective facts and make us deaf to calls for moderation or prudence. Yet to issue these warnings about emotion is not to return to the view that emotions are dangerous irrational forces. Rather, it is to remind us that we have responsibility, individually and collectively, to develop healthy emotional habits, and to learn to use well our emotional "window" on the world, just as we must learn to use well our other faculties.

Notes

1 On dualisms, see Ward, *Objectively Engaged Journalism*, Chapter 1. Also, Putnam, *The Collapse of the Fact-Value Dichotomy*.
2 I provide a full philosophical and historical critique of "objectivity of the hard fact" in *Objectively Engaged Journalism* and *Global Journalism Ethics*.
3 See Bacon, *The New Organon*.
4 See Ayer's *Logical Positivism* for a classic set of articles by logical positivists. On how logical positivism sought to build knowledge up from untainted, pure "bricks" of experience, see Galison's excellent historical account of early positivism, "Aufbau/Bauhaus."
5 At the dawn of modern journalism in the 17th century, editors of the fledgling newsbooks and broadsheets stressed the "impartiality" and factuality of their journalism. In England, editors claimed impartiality in the very titles of their papers, such as *The Faithful Scout, Impartially Communicating*. See Ward, *The Invention of Journalism Ethics*, 131.
6 Gentry, *A Philosophical Life*, 79.
7 Against dualism, see Dewey, *Experience and Nature*, 241. On the spectator theory, see Dewey, *Reconstruction in Philosophy*, 64.
8 In 18th-century England, spectator journalism was made fashionable by the ironic, "civil" observations of the impassioned English public sphere found in Addison and Steele's *Spectator* magazine. See Ward, *The Invention of Journalism Ethics*, 166.
9 See Putnam, *The Collapse of the Fact-Value Dichotomy*.
10 Dewey, *The Public and Its Problems*, 3–8
11 Quine, *Pursuit of Truth*, 13–21.
12 On how experience is mediated by conceptual schemes, see Ward, *The Invention of Journalism Ethics*, 291–296.
13 For my detailed theory of pragmatic objectivity see Chapter 8 of *The Invention of Journalism Ethics*. I sometimes use "holistic objectivity" to bring out the centrality of holism.
14 Haack, *Manifesto of a Passionate Moderate*, 10.
15 Sen, *The Idea of Justice*, 124–152.
16 On the contribution of wonder to the progress of science, see Daston and Park's *Wonders and the Order of Nature*.
17 Dr. Spock is a character from the TV science fiction series, *Star Trek*. The non-human Dr. Spock was frequently baffled by the human insistence on bringing emotions into decisions.
18 See Nussbaum's *Upheavals of Thought: The Intelligence of Emotions*, and *Political Emotions: Why Love Matters to Justice*.
19 Nussbaum, *Upheavals of Thought*, 24, 1, 30
20 Nussbaum, *Upheavals of Thought*, 49
21 Nussbaum, *Political Emotions*, 400
22 Goodman, *Languages of Art*, 248. Italics is in Goodman's text.
23 Goodman, *Languages of Art*, 248.

3 Disrupt detachment – engagement

In Chapter 2, I sought to undermine the philosophical picture of objective knowledge that supported the professional model of journalism. I proposed an alternate model of objectivity that stressed the impartial, holistic testing of interpretations created by engaged agents. I rejected neutrality and an objectivity of hard facts.

In this chapter, I explain how this alternate model applies to journalism. It begins with disrupting detachment and adopting engagement. Good journalism is not defined by neutrality and "just the facts" reporting. It is defined by applying objective methods to an important political purpose – advocacy for egalitarian democracy, and human flourishing, globally.[1] Journalists should be advocates for democracy. They should create and maintain democratic publics through forms of journalism that go far beyond factual stenography, especially in this time of trouble for democracy. The future of pluralistic, egalitarian democracy – the best polity for a global world of media-linked differences – is at stake. Journalists take note: the future of democratic journalism depends on the future of egalitarian democracy.

Section 1: democracy in peril

Need for democratic engagement

For the rest of the book, I propose the ideal of democratically engaged journalists. I start by explaining why this ideal is important.

The main reason is that egalitarian democracy, a democracy that seeks equality as much as freedom, defends the rule of law, protects minority rights from intolerant majorities, and encourages respectful debate, is in peril. The ideal is challenged around the world. Meanwhile, the two ideologies that have shaped journalism in the past – neutral and partisan journalism – are not up to the task of fostering the journalism that democracy requires. We need a special form of engaged journalism which clearly understands the conditions for egalitarian democracy to flourish and is prepared to use the best methods of journalism to promote this political goal. While journalism can (and does) exist without democracy, no form of democracy worth having can exist without a journalism dedicated to democratic principles.

Democracy is a problem for several reasons. The *practice* of democracy, as a working system of government that seeks to be plural and egalitarian, is in deep trouble. The pillars of egalitarian democracy are shaken every day by intolerant voices advancing racism, xenophobia, or representing some form of economic or class privilege. The *ideal* of democracy – a place where citizens deliberate impartially and factually on the common good – fails to guide politics. In the United States and in many other countries, we witness the erosion of democratic communities bound by norms of tolerance, compromise, dialogue, and objective facts. Citizens who disagree with extreme populists are dismissed as unpatriotic citizens.

As I stated in the first chapter, three large factors have created, in large part, this turmoil: (1) the rise of a global public sphere; (2) the rise of extremist populism and its infiltration of mainstream politics; and (3) the rise of information technologies that can be used to spread misinformation, division, and hatred.[2] Despite the creative media unleashed by the digital revolution, the public sphere is corrupted in its capacity to discern truth from falsity, sincere reporters from manipulative voices, experts from ideologues, facts from uninformed assertion. The channels of information that inform democratic citizens – the very lifeblood of democracy – are polluted by false information, conspiracy theories, ideological extremism and manipulative groups.

Testing democracy

Is my view of democracy too negative?

Some American scholars are worried about the leadership of President Trump but they have a rosier overall view of democracy than me. For example, Levitsky and Ziblatt doubt that democracy is declining in the world. They note that the number of democracies grew in the 1980s and 1990s and peaked about 2005. It has remained stable since then.[3] They acknowledge problems in European democracies but say there is "little evidence in any of them of the kind of fundamental erosion of norms we have seen in the United States." Despite "fundamental erosion," they do not believe American democracy will actually fail.

Other experts are not so sanguine.

Larry Diamond, a leading authority on democracy globally, believes the world has entered a period of "democratic recession."[4] The premise of a recent book, *Authoritarianism Goes Global*, by Diamond and others, is that, over the past decade, illiberal powers have grown ever stronger and bolder in the global arena. Leading authoritarian countries – including China, Iran, Russia, Saudi Arabia, and Venezuela – have developed new tools and strategies to contain the spread of democracy, and challenge liberal movements internationally. Undemocratic regimes repress civil society and control cyberspace. At the same time, advanced democracies are failing to respond to the authoritarian threat.[5]

The view that democracy is deeply troubled is supported by recent global studies on the health of democracy. For example, the headline for *The Economist's* 2017 democracy index, released in January 2018, was "Democracy Continues its Disturbing Retreat."[6] According to the index, Norway remains the most democratic country. Western Europe accounted for 14 of the 19 full democracies. The index concluded that the 2017 study "records the worst decline in global democracy in years. Not a single region recorded an improvement in its average score since 2016, as countries grapple with increasingly divided electorates. Freedom of expression in particular is facing new challenges from both state and non-state actors." Less than 5% of the world's population live in a "full democracy." Nearly a third live under authoritarian rule.

In the United States, the Pew Center's polling reveals important trends. Also in January 2018, the center published a poll that found a "deepening anxiety" around the world about the future of democracy. "Emboldened autocrats and rising populists have shaken assumptions about the future trajectory of liberal democracy," the report stated.[7] The 38-nation poll found more than 50% support for representative democracy, yet it *also* found an "openness" to non-democratic forms of government, such as rule by experts (independent of any legislature) and rule by the military. The poll called the commitment to representative democracy "shallow."

A global public sphere

Ironically, a contributor to democracy's problems is something that, at first, looked like a ground-shaking, technological achievement and a boon for democracy. It was the development of a global media based on the internet, accessible to citizens outside of professional journalism.

Global, digital media emerged in the second half of the 1990s but only today are we appreciating its full social and political significance. In the early days, of the late 1900s and early 2000s, digital media were praised as populist, as ending the information control of elite mainstream news media. Journalistic ideals of neutrality, strict verification, and "just the facts" gave way to values of immediacy and opining. Initially, the many voices online were described as a "democratization" of media, leading to "we the media."

More information, more voices online, more "sharing" – is this not the pop-ulist ideal of democracy? What could go wrong?

In recent years, this naïve enthusiasm has waned. The negative, ugly side of digital media dominates the daily headlines. It became clear that online sharing of information and views could be undemocratic, used by elites in government, partisan groups, public relations, or the military. It turned the public sphere into a raucous, sometimes dangerous, global space of trolls, hackers, conspiracy theorists, racists, unwarranted surveillance, and robotic manipulation of social media by governments. The voice of the informed, moderate journalist has diminished, lost in a roiling sea of opinion. Inside their ideological silos, people close their ears to inconvenient facts, and close their hearts to strangers. A new tyranny of angry majorities, full of fear and tribalism, threatens. Citizens wonder what media reports they can trust; civic groups worry that they will not be heard in a democracy of hyper-opinion.

It is nasty out there, on the internet.

Information or misinformation?

Information is power. But misinformation is also power. In 2017, when the BBC's Future Now project interviewed 50 experts on the great challenges of our century, many named the breakdown of trusted information.

In recent years, media scholars have begun to grasp the enormity of the problem. They have moved beyond talking about the biased reports of individual mainstream journalists and their newsrooms. They focus on the global public sphere where misinforming is systematic. These scholars have searched for words to do justice to the trend, calling it "information disor-der,"[8] or "digital deceit."[9] They talk about digital demagogues.[10] Others call ideological global media "computational propaganda" defined as "the use of information and communication technologies to manipulate perceptions, affect cognition, and influence behavior" to manipulate the perceptions of the public and the actions of elected officials.[11]

In *Information Disorder*, Wardle and Derakhshan call the public sphere "a global media environment of information disorder":

> While the historical impact of rumours and fabricated content have been well documented, we argue that contemporary social technology means that we are witnessing something new: information pollution at a global scale; a complex web of motivations for creating, dissemi-nating and consuming these "polluted" messages; a myriad of content types and techniques for amplifying content; innumerable platforms

hosting and reproducing this content; and breakneck speeds of communication between trusted peers.[12]

To appreciate how manipulative the political sphere is today, one only has to watch an undercover investigation by Channel 4 News in Britain, broadcast in early 2018, on how the firm Cambridge Analytica used citizen's personal data in elections.[13] One of the senior executives is taped as saying: "We just put information into the bloodstream of the internet, and then watch it grow, give it a little push every now and again . . . like a remote control. It has to happen without anyone thinking, 'that's propaganda,' because the moment you think 'that's propaganda,' the next question is, 'who's put that out?'"

In our global media sphere, false information spreads more quickly and more extensively than truthful information, a technological proof of the old adage that a lie can travel halfway around the world before the truth can get its boots on. For example, one study at the University of Wisconsin investigated the true and false news stories distributed on Twitter from 2006 to 2017.[14] The data comprise over 126,000 stories tweeted by about 3 million people more than 4.5 million times. The findings? Falsehood diffused significantly farther, faster, deeper, and more broadly than the truth in all categories of information. False news was more novel than true news, which suggests that people were more likely to share novel information.

In "Digital Deceit," Ghosh and Scott argue that sophisticated computer algorithms to gather detailed information on people who are online, developed for marketing and advertising, are now used by political parties, governments, and extreme groups to send messages to citizens through social media, such as the Russian government's use of Facebook to affect elections.[15] As Ghosh and Scott state: "When disinformation operators leverage this system for precision propaganda, the harm to the public interest, the political culture, and the integrity of democracy is substantial."[16]

Section 2: dialogic democracy

Meaning of dialogic democracy

To respond to these ominous trends, we need to be clear about what we oppose and what we support. A firm knowledge of the principles of democracy is useful. For example, a desire to rid the world of fake news can easily become a campaign against free speech. Most important is to have a clear conception of plural, egalitarian, dialogic democracy.

I begin with the long phrase, "plural, egalitarian, dialogic democracy."[17] Pluralism in this context is not simply the fact that modern societies contain groups of many kinds. It is the normative view that pluralism is a *good* feature of societies, providing a diversity of resources, skills, and experiences. Egalitarian democracy seeks a "reasonable pluralism" where groups advance different but reasonable – i.e., rational and informed – perspectives combined with respect for other reasonable views.[18] This pluralism leads to egalitarianism. There should be a rough equality among the plurality of contending groups. Egalitarian democracy seeks equality among citizens on political, social, and economic levels. Equality is a supreme principle of democracy, no less fundamental than freedom. It is both a requirement of justice and a practical necessity for stable, peaceful government over the long term. As Dworkin states: "No government is legitimate that does not show equal concern for the fate of all those citizens over whom it claims dominion and from whom it claims allegiance." Equality is the "sovereign virtue" because, without it, "government is only tyranny," and when a nation's wealth is poorly distributed, "its equal concern is suspect."[19]

Equality, in turn, entails dialogue. Ideally, all citizens should be able to participate in public discussions on matters that affect themselves and their country. For dialogue to occur, participants must adopt two attitudes: First, participants hope that public discussion will *improve* our views and identify common ground. The goal is to arrive at better decisions about the common good for all, not to impose one's ideology on others, or to use communication techniques to undermine other voices. Dialogue is not a monologue. Participants listen, learn, and improve their views in light of the discussion. Dialogue is ethical communication.

Second, the participants adopt an impartial stance toward issues. Ideally, they adopt the stance of pragmatic objectivity. Public dialogue is a cooperative inquiry into a topic from different standpoints, where we partially transcend our situations to listen. We put a critical distance between us and our beliefs. Knowing that social issues are complex, participants take on what Rawls calls the "burdens of judgment": they acknowledge the possibility of other plausible views. They recognize that one's judgment may fail to fit the facts, or one's thinking is flawed, or one's view may be biased by past experience.

It is likely that, at some point, dialogue will bring up fundamental political principles such as appear in the nation's constitution, e.g., principles of free speech, freedom from discrimination, and equality before the law. Here, the dialogic approach is absolutely crucial. Intelligent and productive discussion of issues cannot take place unless groups agree on the principles that define their political association. This agreement is crucial, even if they disagree on other matters, such as religious or metaphysical views about life. Democracy needs an "overlapping consensus" among groups on fundamental principles of justice and rights.[20] An intolerant approach to discourse about these fundamentals destroys hope of an overlapping consensus among reasonable views.

Dialogic democracy, then, is a distinct form of democracy. It is not direct democracy, and it is not expert democracy, where citizens let experts decide matters. It is not a populist government led by a popular "strong" man. Dialogic democracy is participatory democracy but it wants the participation to take the form of reasonable discourse. Dialogic democracy is not a democracy where people have free speech but misuse that freedom to viciously attack others.

Three levels of democracy

Democracy is a great political good. As Dewey argued, democracy is a precondition for the richest kind of communal life and human flourishing.[21] Also, I would argue, dialogic democracy is the highest or fullest form of democracy. Nations must pass through three levels of political development to approach genuine dialogic democracy.

Level 1 is a nation with a minimal democracy where its denizens can consider themselves citizens and not just "subjects" of a king, tyrant, or military junta. Citizens have limited rights to free speech, association, and political participation. The list of rights is meager and the list of duties and restrictive laws is long. Inequalities are obvious and entrenched, and institutions often unjust, tainted by power and conflicts of interest. Such nations have citizens, but the citizens do not form a true public.

Level 2 is a further development of democracy. The list of liberties is longer and better protected, including constitutional protections for both the liberties and the rights of minorities. Inequalities are less evident and reforms seek to bring about egalitarian society. Institutions are more independent and seek to honor principles of justice. Citizens can be called a public since they are effective, to a significant extent, in holding government accountable and, through their interactions, to influence decisions. At its best, Level 2 democracy is a participatory democracy where citizens can speak out publicly and take common action. It is mistakenly thought that participatory democracy, e.g., through the internet, is the best form of democracy. It ignores the importance of *how* people communicate.

Level 3 is a participatory democracy that is egalitarian and dialogic. Much of the participation is tolerant and cooperative. In addition, the society exemplifies democratic community. Institutions and groups are organized around the democratic principles of inclusivity, transparency, and equal participation.

Countries must create Level 1 and Level 2 democracies before they can aspire to Level 3. Most democracies in the world exist somewhere between

Level 1 and Level 2 and move toward or away from Level 1 and Level 2 over time. Every day, people around the world fight to be members of minimal democratic publics. Achieving and maintaining democracy are constant struggles. Among nations approaching Level 3, I would name the countries at the top of the surveys that measure democracy, such as Norway, Sweden, and Canada.

Importance of political culture

Levitsky and Ziblatt argue rightly that, when it comes down to maintaining democracy, unwritten democratic norms are as important as the written rules.[22]

The "written rules" are the laws and formal procedures of institutions necessary for democratic governance, such as rules for legislatures and judicial proceedings. The unwritten rules govern something that is more intangible – people's attitudes and norms. The norms shape how people act toward each other in the political sphere: how they talk to each other, how they reciprocate, how they restrain their desire for power. At question is conduct that goes beyond what the law requires, yet it is crucial for good governance. It is a matter of political morality.

These unwritten norms shape a country's political culture in the same way that unwritten norms shape our social culture, i.e., how we interact with families, friends, and colleagues. A pick-up game of "road hockey" in Canada needs no referees, and no written list of rules. There is unwritten agreement on what constitutes overly aggressive play, what happens when an automobile rumbles down the road, and so on. We *expect* others to honor these norms so cooperation is possible. The same holds when we participate in our political culture. The informal norms of democracy breathe humanity, compassion, and life into the "hard" formal aspects of democratic structures. Agreement on these norms helps institutions work better. Without them, we experience a hollowing out of democracy, until all that is left is an empty shell of public buildings and formal rules. What are the main norms of dialogic democracy?

The main norms

- *Treat each other as free and equal citizens*: Cohen wrote: democracy is a "political society of equals, in which the justification of institutions – as well as laws and policies addressed to consequential problems – involves public argument based on the common reason of members, who regard one another as equals."[23]
- *Act as partners in self-government:* Citizens do not regard political opponents as sworn enemies in the running of our country.

- *Value democratic processes*: Citizens support the messy, time-consuming process of representational democracy and regard public deliberation as intrinsically valuable.
- *Adopt the objective stance*: Citizens are willing to step back and critique their views, seek evidence, and fairly compare positions.
- *Develop a deep understanding of one's democracy:* Citizens understand their governing political principles and challenge misinterpretations.
- *Display political courage and responsibility*: Citizens, including politicians, need courage to oppose extreme measures and to isolate demagogues.
- *Expand democratic culture beyond politics:* Citizens introduce democratic processes to the running of schools and civic meetings, to the governance of corporations and institutions.

Section 3: democratically engaged journalism

Understating engagement

During the heyday of news objectivity, in the mainstream press of the mid-1900s, the engaged nature of much reporting was understated, if not denied. Journalism codes spoke of the duties of journalists to the public and to justice, but such duties were *not* identified as forms of social engagement or advocacy – the bête noire of professional objectivism. To the contrary, journalists were supposed to maintain an editorial "wall" between themselves and sources, and advertisers. Independence required detachment or "distance" from actors in the public sphere. These actors, it was feared, might corrupt a reporter's virtue – his neutrality. Therefore, a tension existed between the lofty social goals of journalism that were named in the preamble of codes and the stern requirements of neutrality listed in the body of the codes. The tension existed in the very rationale for neutral reporting. Why should journalists accept the restraints of neutrality and objectivity of hard facts? The ethical reason was that neutral reporting provided unbiased information for the public. But, why is this important? Because journalism has a goal to advocate: to better inform self-governing citizens. But isn't this commitment the same as being engaged in society, i.e., following neutrality to achieve social goals? It was not clear.

What is clear is that journalists, neutral or not, have always had goals. Historically, journalists have been engaged in society as reformists, revolutionaries, columnists with a political agenda, or hosts of TV news programs that critique and comment. Even when journalists stick to reporting, forms of engagement emerge to give the reporting a greater purpose than simply chronicling events. For example, war reporters report to warn the world about the evil nature of a regime and an impending genocide; reporters draw the world's attention to famine or human rights violations; reporters investigate abuses of power that harm ordinary people. Engagement of some kind seems irrepressible, and often desirable. Therefore, I believe we journalists should be frank and say we *are* engaged socially. Then, develop a philosophy of journalism from this starting point.

Democratically engaged journalists are advocates because to protect and advance anything is, by definition, to advocate. But they practice an advocacy of a certain kind. They are *objective advocates* of egalitarian democracy and the flourishing of their publics. They practice an informed and fair advocacy for the common good. This advocacy is different from the partisan advocacy for a group or ideology. It is opposed to an extreme partisanship that would use any manipulative means of persuasion. Democratically engaged journalists see their methods as means to a larger political goal – providing accurate, verified interpretations of events and policies as the necessary informational base for democracy. Democratic journalists seek to be objective public informers and dialogue generators *within* an overarching commitment to egalitarian democracy.

Neutral or partisan?

Given that egalitarian democracy is at stake, disengagement by citizen or journalist is not an ethical option. We must do more than shake our heads at the fake news bounding across the global internet, or simply feel anxious for democracy. Journalists and citizens need to figure out how democratic media should respond to the challenges.

In the United States, faced with an erratic, media-bashing president, some mainstream journalists call on reporters to remain neutral and return to basic principles such as reporting just the facts. To "double down" on the traditional norms of objective reporting. Ironically, a good number of journalists, after decades of skepticism about objectivity, want to revive a journalism of facts. Others call for a partisan, anti-Trump media.

Truly, these are confused times.

We should not go back to the idea of journalists as neutral stenographers of fact or as overt partisans. We need to find another way forward.

A journalism of just the facts is too passive and ripe for manipulation. In a partisan public sphere, what *is* a fact is up for debate, and requires active investigation. In such a climate, a democratically engaged journalism must not be a neutral spectator or channel of information that merely repeats people's alleged facts. Critical evaluation and informed interpretation motivated by a clear notion of the goal of democratic media are essential. A studied neutrality is a luxury we cannot afford today when powerful groups practice journalism for their own benefit. Being a neutral stenographer of alleged facts is not the goal of journalism. Impartiality in service of democratic engagement is the correct goal. Nor will partisanship help. If journalists join the protesters, it will erode media credibility and contribute to an already partisan-soaked media sphere. It will give populists and others evidence for their mantra that the "media" (as a whole) is biased and the generators of fake facts

I propose we think of journalism as lying between partisan advocacy and mincing neutrality. Some people will rightly say there must be a third way between being neutral and being partisan. There must be a view of journalism that allows journalists to be factual yet not simply repeat the dubious "factual" assertions of leaders. Surely, there is a "middle" way or a hybrid conception of good journalism that is both impartial and engaged. But many of these citizens would be hard-pressed to say *what* that ethic of objective engagement is. Democratically engaged journalism is a third way.

Neutrality and engagement

In Chapter 2, we saw how objectivity and engagement are compatible in general, and in many professions. How are they compatible in journalism? In the same way. They are compatible because of the difference between means and goals. The norms that help us report impartially, e.g., accuracy and verification, help us to be properly engaged, to achieve certain goals and perform certain functions. Impartiality and objectivity are not self-sufficient stances. They make sense relative to a larger set of purposes, a non-neutral engagement with the world.

Democratically engaged journalists have a dual commitment. They are committed to impartial methods as a means to their partial commitment to egalitarian democracy. They commit themselves to holistic objectivity – to rational and objective methods for deciding what to publish and how to persuade. They are motivated by rational passions.

Neutrality is an entrenched misunderstanding of modern journalism ethics. Historically, journalists have never been able to practice strict neutrality with any consistency. Also, among the best examples of journalism are non-neutral investigations. Were the editors of the *Washington Post* neutral when they opposed Nixon as he tried to prevent the publication of the *Pentagon Papers?* Many codes of ethics appeal to the social goals of journalism: to serve a public, to reveal wrong-doing and injustice, to unearth the truth about some person or agency who lies and conceals facts. When journalism societies give out awards for excellence, the judges stress how the journalists gave voice to the voiceless, or stopped injustice, or enhanced democracy. Neutrality is not stressed.

Journalists, whether they wish to affirm it or not, are goal-driven agents who interpret events. They interpret according to their conceptual schemes. Think about an insightful journalistic report of a high court's ruling on a constitutional problem, based on the journalist's research. Think about an accurate journalistic report on a complex event, such as a fierce debate in Parliament. Both reports are interpretations, not simply recitations of "just the facts." The journalists select the facts they deem most important; they choose the story angle, they choose which sources and which quotes to include, and they decide that certain claims are questionable. They interpret the event according to the point of their practice, the journalist styles and protocols that shape their work and writing, and their interpretation of what is significant. Journalists interpret even where their reports are based on events that happen right before them and do not involve high theory or speculation.

Plural journalism, plural needs

The issue for an engaged philosophy of journalism comes down to two large questions: (1) journalistic engagement for what and for whom? And, (2) what types of journalism promote this engagement?

My answer to the first question is: *journalism should promote plural, egalitarian, dialogic democracy, locally and globally, since dialogic democracy is intimately related to human freedom, justice and flourishing.*[24] My answer to the second question is: *forms of journalism should be judged by the extent to which they meet the crucial media needs of a robust democratic public.*

The general standard, then, is having significant democratic value. This standard recognizes the following as valid forms: reporting and investigative journalism, explanatory journalism, participatory journalism and dialogic journalism. Principled pluralism excludes unethical applications of these major forms of journalism, such as inaccurate reporting, uninformed explanatory journalism, and a disrespectful opinion journalism that maligns other views. The dialogic approach distinguishes between valuable opinion journalism and non-valuable opinion journalism when we consider the needs of democracy. This is important at a time of increasingly partisan and intolerant journalism. Dialogic theory believes the most valuable form of opinion journalism is a *moderate* opinion journalism that brings forward a diversity of positions for reasonable public scrutiny.

The public needs many types of information and communication, beyond straight factual reporting. Consider the types of information in Figure 3.1. I identify six kinds of "media needs" in a democracy: (1) factual reporting and in-depth investigations; (2) explanatory journalism, such as we find in

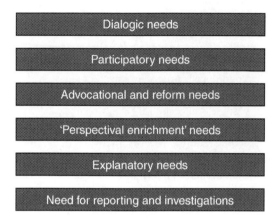

Figure 3.1 What the public needs

science journalism; (3) exposure to a wide variety of informed perspectives to enhance perspectives; (4) reform and advocacy journalism; (5) a media system where citizens can participate in doing journalism and in media discussions; and (6) dialogic forms of media discussion, not ranting.

Traditionally, the professional model of neutral journalism has privileged one of those needs – the bottom square, representing factual, information needs. But once you admit the other five needs, you introduce ways of doing journalism that go beyond fact-stating. You place value on a journalism that involves explicit interpretation, the reasoned sharing of views, historical and causal explanations, knowledge of the values of one's society, and their links to global issues.

Promoting dialogic democracy

In Chapter 5, I discuss the many things that journalists and citizens should do to defend dialogic democracy. Here, I mention two items related to promoting a dialogic public. Democratically engaged journalists should honor two duties:

Duty 1: dialogic journalism

Journalists have a duty to convene public fora and provide channels of information that allow for frank but respectful dialogue across divisions. They should seek to mend the tears in the fabric of the body politic. They should work against, in an advocacy role, the trend that sees confrontation replace reasonable discussion; and fear of the "other" replace an openness to humanity. Dialogic journalism challenges racial and ethnic stereotypes and policies, e.g., investigating the factual basis of new immigration (and other) laws. It means opposing the penchant to demonize. It means exposing the perpetrators and supporters of hate speech.

Whether a dialogue occurs depends not only on the speakers but on the manner in which their encounter in the media is structured. A heavy ethical burden lies on the shoulders of media producers, editors, and hosts to design dialogic encounters. We are all too familiar with the provocative "journalists" who seek ratings through disrespectful ranting and heated confrontation with guests. But we also have good dialogic examples such as public-issue shows on public television where viewpoints are critiqued on the basis of facts, not on the basis of the ethnicity or personal details of the speaker.

Duty 2: go deep politically

However, fostering the right sort of democracy-building conversations is not enough. Conversations need to be well-informed. This is where the second duty arises. Journalism needs to devote major resources to an explanatory journalism that delves deeply into the political values, processes, and institutions of egalitarian democracy, while challenging the myths and fears surrounding issues such as immigration, terrorism, and so on. There is a movement towards fact-checking web sites. It is a good idea but insufficient. It is not enough to know that a politician made an inaccurate statement. Many citizens need a re-education in liberal democracy. They will be called on soon to judge issues that depend on civic knowledge. A democracy without a firm grasp on its principles is flying blind.

Section 4: skepticism and objections

I have explained how objectivity and engagement are compatible in general and in journalism due to the distinction of means and ends. But skepticism remains. Additional queries arise about facts, emotions, and attachments in journalism. I attempt to answer these questions.

Journalism beyond facts

Does talk of engaged journalism undermine the belief in facts, or the importance of facts in reporting?

No, it does not. Pragmatic objectivity does not share a post-modern skepticism that there are no truths or facts, or that we entirely "construct" facts.

Construction must have some materials with which to work. It is inconsistent to ask us to accept the truth that there is no truth. If we moderns are so sophisticated that we "see through" all sincere attempts to express truth as naïve, or as disguised projections of power or bias, then why should we inquire or deliberate? As C. S. Lewis said, the whole point of "seeing through something" – i.e., to critique and analyze something – is to see something else, to grasp some deeper truth: "To 'see through' all things is the same as not to see."[25]

Facts help us to see things. They are important not just to reporters but also to investigative journalists in their efforts to expose government corruption. Pragmatic objectivity protects the importance of facts in a postmodern age by giving us a defensible understanding of their role in the economy of human thought. To wit: they are important criteria of evaluation for interpretations, and they force us to confront reality. Yet pragmatic objectivity also reminds us that, as Bacon knew, the task of knowing facts is a complex process. For example, facts in journalism need context to make sense and to be useful. Government statistics about the rate of unemployment and police "facts" about how well they are fighting crime in their community should not be accepted (or reported) at face value. Journalists should use statistical (and other) methods to interpret the data. In health reporting, journalists should compare the cancer rate of a group in a clinical trial with background levels of cancer in the general population. In political reporting, the "facts" of opinion polls are worthless unless correctly interpreted. Often, getting the correct interpretation of the facts is as important as knowing the "bare" facts. Journalists also need to carefully select facts for relevance and importance and organize them into coherent patterns. In an era of "big data" – computerized methods for ascertaining patterns in mammoth amounts of data – journalists need to be skilled interpreters of data. Engaged journalists are not stenographers of alleged fact, but they are avid investigators into fact – important, revealing fact.

Having reserved an important place for factual claims, I now state something that may sound like heresy to objective journalists. While fact-checking is important to good journalism, we need a journalism beyond facts. Not journalism without facts. But an interpretive journalism that is informed, but not reducible, to facts. We need journalistic sherpas helping citizens to navigate through a miasma of shock talk, trolls, and partisan diatribe by analyzing the meaning of events and the motivations of the political players. We need journalists with the cultural knowledge and critical skills to create credible interpretations of events *and* critique other people's views. A journalism beyond facts displays a healthy respect and appetite for empirical fact and our best empirical theories. But it does not seek to be neutral or to reduce narratives to facts scrubbed clean of all interpretation.

In many cases, the problem is not that the public have the wrong facts. They have the wrong principles – or, to be precise, a wrong understanding of principles. For example, they misunderstand the political principles involved in a debate over free speech or the independency of the judiciary. Many disputes involve someone's dubious, self-serving interpretation of principle, e.g., the way America's National Rifle Association has fostered a mythical and incorrect view of the US Constitution's 2nd Amendment, or the right to bear arms. US citizens may misunderstand the importance of the First Amendment when a president threatens to remove the license of a major broadcaster because of critical stories. Journalists create informed citizens not only by supplying them with facts. They inform them by "going deep" politically – by discussing the meaning and scope of the political principles which apply to current disputes. Pragmatic objectivity is flexible enough to provide standards that help journalists test not only facts but interpretations of principle.

Disrupt subjectivism: assessing values

Journalists are necessarily entangled with judgments of value. Journalists evaluate. Is the prime minister's initiative to stimulate the economy of real value? Will it produce the desired consequences? The daily news is full of value judgments – tales of winners and losers, good guys and bad guys. Reporters cannot avoid evaluative language in reporting on unfair bosses, brutal massacres, vicious murders, notorious pedophiles, and dangerous terrorists. Journalists employ evaluations in selecting credible sources or displaying skepticism towards a new scientific theory. To enter journalism is to enter a value-laden craft in a value-laden public sphere. New journalists learn more than the skills of writing news and gathering information. They acculturate into a realm of reporting routines, news values, and peer attitudes.

In addition, responsible journalists follow ethical principles and values. These values come from either the general morality of society or they come from codes of journalism ethics. They follow norms that express the values of their practice, such as accuracy, minimizing harm, acting independently, and promoting democracy. Journalism ethicists have developed methods for "doing" journalism ethics, i.e., practical models of how to apply principles to situations. The models help journalists weigh and balance values.

So when journalists, working ethically, confront the widespread view that values are inherently subjective judgments that bias factual inquiry, they can be excused for feeling bemused or for sensing an air of unreality around such a philosophical view. Easy to say all values are subjective, but how does *that* help reporters to make difficult decisions? Reporters work hard to steer the ship of journalism in an ethical direction, but the subjectivists ride for free.

The first step is to set aside this extreme subjectivism or relativism. We set it aside by granting the subjectivist every theoretical premise they desire, and then pointing out that the task of ethics remains, pragmatically. For example, let us grant that there is no one, uniquely objective, system of ethics that describes moral facts; let us grant that a certain amount of relativity affects any evaluation, e.g., any judgment is relative to a set of ethical values, of which there are many; let us even grant that every person in the world has their "own" set of values, as is common asserted, implausibly. I now ask, where does this leave us? Just where we began. Ethics is a practical enterprise in which humans must engage, no matter how imperfect or relative our morals might appear, from a theoretical standpoint. People have different values, but if they wish to live together, and if they wish to practice a profession in a social setting, they must at some point agree on *some* norms and values. The entire point of ethics is to find fair rules for social cooperation, no matter what the theoretical status of those rules is.

Journalists cannot use subjectivism to escape from doing ethics because their actions impact society. They need to articulate values that earn the support of most citizens. Ethics is the attempt to find an overlap of values to make society, or some part of society, possible. Ethical principles are proposals for fair rules of social engagement.[26] People adopt the objective stance not to know a separate moral reality but to make reasonable practical decisions. Those proposals may be useful and valid even if they are not absolute propositions. The key issue for an ethical proposal, e.g., some rule, is not whether it is true to reality but whether the proposal is pragmatically useful, i.e., has good consequences and is fair (or just).

Subjectivism ignores how much agreement is possible among reasonable people if they can agree on principles of fair cooperation. In society, most people agree on what Gert called the "common morality" – such as the belief that murder is wrong, that people should keep promises, that people should avoid causing harm to others, and that people should help others in distress.[27] In journalism, given a common code of ethics, journalists can rationally evaluate decisions and have rational debates. Not everything is subjective. The principles of the common morality and of professional codes do evolve, are rarely completely unanimous, and are not perfectly objective. But within plausible value systems, rational and objective judgments can be made. In fact, such judgments *must* be made, practically, to the best of our ability. The only other option would be to make decisions randomly or in a purely self-interested manner.

If we look at how we actually live as agents in society, we can see how ludicrous and unhelpful it is to claim that we cannot rationally evaluate our values and decisions. When young, did I not carefully evaluate whether I should become a jazz trumpet player or a philosopher? I did. Do we not evaluate the consequences of two courses of action, such as going to war or not? Do we not look to facts, rights, and other factors to assess whether I have a duty to take care of my aging mother at home, rather than place her in a nursing home? Do responsible journalists not do the same when confronted by their dilemmas? To dump all of these important rational evaluative activities into the trash can of "subjective values" is to forget that philosophical theories should help us understand our everyday existence, not explain it away.

The good news is that there are better or worse ways of valuing and testing our values. One way is to apply the test of holistic objectivity, adopting the objective stance, and evaluating our belief or decision according to sets of standards, as outlined in Chapter 2. In Chapter 5, I will explain how this method can be used in journalism.

Ranking attachments

Perhaps value judgments can be treated objectively, but what about attachments or loyalties to people and groups? If journalists are loyal to certain groups, doesn't this create a bias or a conflict of interest?

I have already suggested what my answer will be. All people have biases, attachments, emotions, and partialities. But that doesn't mean such things are necessarily biasing and negative. My partiality to my family may prompt me to jump into a raging river to save my son; or my partiality to a friend may prompt me to come to his aid in distress. We would not wish to eliminate such partialities, even if we could. Yet, my loyalty to Canada, and its interests, may lead me to ignore unjust foreign initiatives in the developing world. The same applies to journalism. A journalist's attachment to struggling refugees in his city may lead him to write stories about their plight. On the other hand, a journalist's attachment to an environmental group may lead them to report in uncritical, glowing terms about their actions.

In the past, attachment in journalism was likely to be called advocacy or activist journalism. Today, advocacy journalism could be a gay newspaper in Vancouver that advocates against discriminatory marriage laws. Or, it could be an online site in New York that supports the Jewish community. Advocacy journalism gets a bad press in some quarters of journalism, particularly from the supporters of neutral, professional reporting. The latter complains that advocates produce journalism that is biased, that twists or ignores facts. It is true that attachments may cause bias. But so can many other things. Almost any form of journalism can be biased or misused, including neutral fact-reporting. Journalists who have attachments are not necessarily biased. Everything depends on *how* they define their goals and *how* they seek them.

What, then, is the difference between democratically engaged journalism and advocacy journalism, or partisan journalism? Recall that, in my view, journalists are social advocates of egalitarian democracy at home and abroad. They value a factual, impartial journalism of *method* for partial ends – democratic goals. This civic engagement is not identical with traditional forms of activist journalism. Democratically engaged journalism has a wider attachment than activism journalism. It promotes the largest social group in the nation, the citizens or the public at large. Engaged journalism is a *wide* reformist journalism whose overall goal is the improvement of democratic civic life for all. Activist and advocacy journalists also have attachments, but they typically promote sub-groups within the public.

Advocacy and activist journalism are important forms of journalism. They contribute to the plural forms of journalism that a public needs, as discussed above. They bring additional perspectives and facts to the public's awareness, and they call attention to overlooked problems.

I support such journalism with one major proviso: that they carry out this journalism properly. What does "properly" mean? It means properly, according to the tenants and goals of democratically engaged journalism. This involves at least two things. First, the activist journalists report on their favored groups and causes in a manner that uses, or at least does not violate, the norms of holistic objectivity. Despite their attachments, activist journalists must be devoted to truth-telling, independence, capable of stepping back to review their beliefs, and willing to follow facts and logic where they lead. They should seek to be impartial in method, despite their partiality to a group. Second, the activist journalist should make loyalty to the public at large their primary and most comprehensive attachment. Do they advance egalitarian, dialogic democracy while advocating for specific groups?

What democratically engaged journalism requires is that journalists *rank* their attachments, or loyalties, in a certain manner. Journalists make their attachment to democratic publics *primary*. It regulates and trumps their attachments to more specific groups. There is, in attached journalism, the danger that bias towards one's specific group may override one's fundamental duty to inform the general public. Partisan and extreme activist journalists may be willing to depart from the standards of holistic objectivity where it advances their specific cause. If the advocacy takes the form of cheap rhetoric, blatant bias, or partisan propaganda, or the denial of inconvenient facts, then it is unethical journalism.

I conclude this chapter with a reflection on emotions, or passions, in journalism. Democratically engaged journalism has a more positive view of emotions than the traditional professional model. It incorporates the view of emotions in Chapter 2. Emotions are not reducible to irrational impulses. They can have cognitive functions. They help us know the world and pay attention to aspects we might ignore. This is especially true in journalism. Feelings of injustice can motivate courageous journalism, and empathy can prompt journalists to pay attention to people in distress. The issue, as I have said, is to be attentive to the emotions we have as journalists and develop healthy habits of emotions.

The best journalism is a judicious blend of two fundamental, rational passions: the passion for important stories for the democratic public; and a passion for objectivity, or objective testing, to ensure accurate and well-verified stories. Reason and passion cooperate.

Notes

1 I deal with the global aspect of journalism reform in the next chapter.
2 For my detailed views on what journalists should do to combat extreme populism, see *Ethical Journalism in a Populist Age*.
3 Levitsky and Ziblatt, *How Democracies Die*, 205.
4 See Diamond's 2015 article, "Facing Up to the Democratic Recession" at www.pewglobal.org or at www.journalofdemocracy.org/sites/default/files/Diamond-26-1_0.pdf
5 Diamond, "Facing Up to the Democratic Recession," 142, 154.
6 The Economist evaluated 167 countries on a scale of 0 to 10 based on 60 indicators.
7 See "Globally, Broad Support for Representative and Direct Democracy," at www.pewglobal.org/2017/10/16/globally-broad-support-for-representative-and-direct-democracy/. Research by Richard Wike, Katie Simmons, Bruce Stokes, and Janell Fetterolf, published on October 16, 2017.
8 Wardle and Derakhshan, "Information Disorder."
9 Ghosh and Scott, "Digital Deceit."
10 See Fuchs, *Digital Demagogue*.
11 See https://prezi.com/b_vewutjwzut/computational-propaganda/
12 Wardle and Derakhshan, "Information Disorder," 4.
13 The reporters filmed the meetings at London hotels over four months, between November 2017 and January 2018. An undercover reporter for Channel 4 News posed as a fixer for a wealthy client hoping to get candidates elected in Sri Lanka.
14 At https://uwmadison.app.box.com/v/TwitterExploit.
15 Ghosh and Scott, "Digital Deceit."
16 Ghosh and Scott, "Digital Deceit," 3.
17 For my full view of dialogic democracy see *Global Journalism Ethics* and *Radical Media Ethics*.
18 Rawls, *Political Liberalism*, 36–37.
19 Rawls's claim that justice, as fairness, is the "first virtue of social institutions, as truth is of systems of thought" is similar in spirit to Dworkin's primacy of equality. Dworkin, *Sovereign Virtue*, 1–3; and Rawls, *A Theory of Justice*, 3.
20 Rawls, *Political Liberalism*, 150–154.
21 Dewey, *Democracy and Education*, 16

22 Levitsky and Ziblatt, *How Democracies Die*, 8.
23 Cohen, *The Arc of the Moral Universe and Other Essays*, 1.
24 This civic sense of engagement is different from a popular use of "engagement" to refer to attracting large audiences to one's web site or online news publication. See Batsell, *Engaged Journalism*.
25 Lewis, *The Abolition of Man*, 67.
26 I explain this pragmatic view of ethics in *Radical Media Ethics* and *Global Journalism Ethics*.
27 See Gert, *Common Morality*.

4   Disrupt patriotism – globalism

Advocating for egalitarian democracy is not the ultimate aim of journalism and ethics. This political goal is of great importance. But there is a larger goal beyond the interests of our nation. It is the interests of humanity. Advocacy of humanity I call globalism.

Our disruptions would be incomplete is we lacked a global aim for global news media. Globalism is advocacy for human flourishing, a loyalty to mankind that crosses borders. Our patriotic attachment to nation plays a lesser role in a global journalism ethic. We disrupt patriotism and its biasing effect on reporting.

Is promoting egalitarian democracy not a form of patriotism? Yes, it is. However, as I explain, it should be a moderate form of patriotism restrained by a prior commitment to global values. Journalists need a broad and clear view of how they serve their country. Also, they need a method for assessing claims that journalists should do x to be patriotic. As with disrupting neutrality, disrupting patriotism requires a critique of assumptions. I argue that journalists should adopt globalism as a moral ideology and become global patriots for human flourishing.

PATRIOTISM AS THE MASTER NORM

Patriotism is a serious and long-standing problem for journalism ethics. The problem is serious because patriotism is an emotion-laden loyalty that may prompt journalists to practice their craft unethically. It may cause journalists to promote extreme nationalism or violate their duties of truth-telling when reporting on issues affecting their nation. Acting as "patriots first, journalists second," journalists may misinform the public, maintain public support for an unjust war, or reduce their criticism of leaders.

The problem is long-standing because the conditions that prompt journalists to report in questionable patriotic ways are as old and permanent as journalism itself – the desire of leaders to have a compliant news media; the emotional commitment of journalists to their country; and the expectation of many citizens that journalists will act as patriotic reporters when their country comes into conflict or competition with other nations. Group loyalties, such as extreme nationalism, are notorious for causing bias. In an era of Net populism, the means of spreading a narrow patriotism are multiplied and strengthened.

We might dismiss patriotism as a secondary issue causing a lapse in journalists' ethical conduct only here and there, if it were not for two unfortunate facts: first, the ethical aberrations caused by patriotism are not "here and there" but plentiful and recurring. The history of modern journalism contains many examples of how the pressure to act as a patriotic citizen compromised the principles of truth-telling, objectivity, and verification. For instance, the history of war reporting is largely a history of uncritical patriotic journalism.[1]

Second, patriotism has been, since the advent of modern news publication, the *master norm* of journalism ethics. By master norm, I mean that, in practice, patriotism is fundamental among the values of journalists. Patriotism trumps other values, where they conflict. Patriotism should not be understood as the intrusion into journalism of an external social value. Patriotism, from the beginning, has been part of the very idea of public journalism.

A commitment to patriotism is an implied premise of many codes of journalism ethics. In the early 1900s, the first explicit codes justified the practice of journalism in terms of serving the public through information and investigation. But the codes, then and today, do not make explicit that serving the public means serving only, or primarily, a *specific* public, the public of a nation. Canadian journalists serve the Canadian public. Australian journalists serve Australians. Such service is done for love of country. In codes, the master norm lies just below the surface – below the high-minded appeals to impartial truth-telling. In times of social division or threat, journalism's commitment to the master norm of patriotism reveals itself.

An objective analysis of patriotism is challenging because of the many forms of patriotism and because of disagreement over the value of patriotism. Some writers argue that patriotism is an emotional attachment to concrete and parochial objects, such as one's native soil and customs. Others argue that patriotism is (or should be) a rational affirmation of broad political principles, such as liberty and equality. Others say it is time to move away from national patriotism toward a cosmopolitan loyalty to humanity.[2]

Moreover, patriotism is a contested value.

Some praise patriotism as a primary civic virtue that binds a society together. Critics reply that patriotism can be aggressive and xenophobic.

More than 100 million people were killed in patriotic wars during the last century. Tolstoy wrote: "Seas of blood have been shed over this passion [of patriotism] and will yet be shed for it, unless the people free themselves of this obsolete relic of antiquity."[3] Therefore, is patriotism an unruly emotion or an essential civic attitude? Do appeals to patriotism carry ethical weight, and, if so, how much?

Yet, despite its importance, there is not a lot of systematic writing on patriotism in journalism ethics.[4] Public debate is sparked by, and confined to, specific controversies. Journalists are accused of acting unpatriotically when they question their country's participation in a particular war, or when they publish classified state documents leaked by whistleblowers. Discussion can be unenlightening. Whether someone condemns or praises a report (or a leak) often depends on whether the report helps that person's political party, or not. The discussion fails to probe deeper questions, such as, what type of patriotism is appropriate for journalists?

Section 1: forms of patriotism

Patriotism is a group loyalty. It is a loyalty to, and love of, one's country or nation. Patriotism is parochial. It is a love of country as *my* country. In drawing a line between what belongs to *us* (co-nationals) and what belongs to foreigners, I draw a political boundary between nations.

Nathanson defines patriotism as "a special affection for, identification with, and a concern for one's own nation and a willingness to act on its behalf." It is "positive commitment to act on one's country's behalf in ways that one would not normally act for other countries."[5] For instance, one is ready to die for one's country but not for another country. Nussbaum defines the political emotions as emotions which "take as their object the nation, the nation's goals, its institutions and leaders, its geography, and one's fellow citizens"[6] Patriotism is a political emotion par excellence. My nation and its interests are more important to me than other nations and their interests. It is one reason citizens in a country can be less concerned about distressed foreigners than distressed co-nationals.

Patriotism: object and strength

One way to categorize forms of patriotism is to distinguish them according to the object of their loyalty and according to the strength of that loyalty.

The main object of patriotism has been communal or political. Communal patriotism is love of the non-political or communal aspects of a society: a loyalty to one's country because of its beautiful land, peoples, languages, and customs. Communal patriotism is concrete, emotive, and folksy, based on personal ties to specific peoples and places. Communal patriotism existed before the modern nation state and nationalism. Political patriotism is the love of one's country's political leader, the state, or its political values and institutions, such as democracy. One loves one's country because it realizes certain political values. Political patriotism is usually more abstract, symbolic, and rational. It is an attachment to principles, laws, and ideals. Political patriotism is expressed in many ways, such as swearing allegiance to a political constitution. Political patriots may support an authoritarian, socialist, or democratic form of government.

Pure forms of political and communal patriotism are rare. Across the centuries, forms of communal and political patriotism have evolved and mingled.[7] The difference between communal and political patriotism is a matter of degree. It depends on which aspect receives the most emphasis. Habermas has argued that, after the Holocaust, only a non-communal, political form of patriotism could be valid in Germany since communal forms had supported Hitler's fanaticism. It must be a "patriotism of the Constitution" based on universal political principles of liberty and democracy embodied in the constitution of the Federal Republic of Germany.[8] Viroli and Nussbaum have replied that the concrete emotions of communal patriotism cannot be ignored. These emotions should be socially cultivated to support non-fanatical patriotism.

Forms of patriotism also differ according to the strength of the attachment to their object. We can place the kinds of patriotism on a continuum with extreme patriotism on one end and weak patriotism on the other end. Moderate patriotism lies between these extremes.

Extreme patriotism includes: (1) a special affection for one's country as *superior* to others; (2) an *exclusive* concern for one's country's well-being and few constraints on the pursuit of one's country's interests; and (3) automatic or *uncritical support* for one's country's actions. Extreme patriotism takes a narrow or often prejudicial attitude towards other nations and cultures. It prepares the ground for extreme nationalism until both are barely distinguishable. Weak patriotism maintains that patriotism is not an important value.

Moderate patriotism is a moderate loyalty to one's country. It consists of: (1) a special affection for one's country; (2) a desire that one's country flourishes and prospers; (3) a special but not exclusive concern for one's country; (4) support for a morally constrained pursuit of national goals; and (5) conditional and critical support of one's country's actions.[9] In other words, moderate patriotism seeks to affirm a love of country but in a way that avoids superiority, exclusivity, and pressure to support one's country uncritically. The loyalty is genuine but limited. Moderate patriots have an inclusive attitude towards other nations. They eschew exaggerating the uniqueness and superiority of their country.

The strength of the emotional attachment is, for many people, conversely related to the distance or abstractness of the object in question. We struggle to be emotionally attached to distant people and abstract philosophical principles. Emotional appeals for foreign aid for strangers may have a temporary and wavering effect. Empathy, compassion, and care "start at home," and, unfortunately, they often stay at home, ignoring those beyond our borders.

Moderate, democratic patriotism

The ethically preferred form of nation-based patriotism is a moderate, inclusive patriotism. I believe this moderate love of country should be mainly political: love of one's country insofar as it embodies the features of egalitarian democracy. For brevity, I call this democratic patriotism. Democratic patriotism is not identical with love of a leader or the state. It is love of a society dedicated to the flourishing of citizens under liberal democratic principles and institutions. Democratic patriotism makes principles primary. The principles are rational restraints on our communal attachments to a *volk*, a fatherland, or a race.

Democratic patriotism has three main components, which originate in the idea of dialogic democracy discussed in Chapter 3. First, a love of democratic political structure: the principles, institutions, and laws that secure liberties and self-government for citizens. Second, a love of dialogic democracy. i.e., meaningful political participation by informed and deliberative citizens. Third, a love of the diffusion of liberal democratic values into the non-political areas of society. Freedom, equality, transparency, and openness characterize the manner in which citizens associate in the many domains of society, from scientific inquiry to the professions.

The values of moderate, democratic patriotism run directly against the values of extreme patriotism. Moderate democratic patriotism stresses tolerance for other cultures, and an openness to criticism. It agrees with Spanish philosopher Ortega y Gasset that, in a democracy, "criticism is patriotism."[10] In short, democratic patriotism is attachment to the values of the democratic political culture described in Chapter 3.

Why prioritize the political? Because as Tolstoy and Habermas warn, a purely emotive, communal love of one's country is a potentially dangerous loyalty, vulnerable to excess and the rhetoric of undemocratic demagogues. As a war reporter, I witnessed, and grew to fear, a communal, nationalistic patriotism of "blood and belonging" that is not restrained by principle and rationality.[11] Moreover, an extreme patriotism, in time, undermines the liberal principles of equality and tolerance, leading to an illiberal populist democracy, a tyranny of the powerful or the majority. To be a democratic patriot, it is not necessary to deny personal affection for one's country. But it is important to constantly subject that affection to scrutiny.

The application of this approach to journalism is straight-forward. We make moderate democratic patriotism the form of patriotism appropriate to journalism, and resist patriotic claims that violate it. Assume that, as a citizen, I commit myself to democratic patriotism. Also, assume that I am a journalist committed to ethical standards. How compatible are these two commitments? They are largely compatible *if* journalists subscribe to moderate democratic patriotism. The principles of democratic journalism are largely compatible with the principles of democratic patriotism because both share the goal of democratic community. Democratic journalism and democratic patriotism share a substantial overlap of values such as freedom, openness, and tolerance. The democratic patriot and the democratic journalist will be on the same side of a number of public issues: both will support accurate, unbiased information; free speech; a critical news media; and a public sphere with diverse perspectives. Both will favor the protection of liberties, transparency in public affairs, and the evaluation of appeals to patriotism. Strong or extreme patriotism is largely incompatible with democratic journalism because it tends to support editorial limits on the press, or it exerts pressure on journalists to be uncritical, partisan, or economical with the truth.

Claims of patriotism

How does one use the idea of democratic patriotism to evaluate specific claims of patriotism, as they arise in practice?

People claim that, in situation *s*, patriots should do *x* or *y*; or the government should do *m* or *n*. Examples of claims of patriotism are: patriots do not allow fellow citizens to burn the national flag; patriots defend the constitution; patriots discourage criticism of the nation's decision to go to war; officials who leak confidential state documents to the media are traitors.

Journalists should use four general criteria for evaluating a claim of patriotism:

1   Compatibility with general morality

A claim to patriotism should be compatible with Gert's "common morality," discussed in Chapter 3, from avoiding harm to not lying. Also, a claim of patriotism should be consistent with the political morality of egalitarian democracy such as respecting equality before the law and the freedom to criticize officials. On these grounds, a claim that journalists should not tell the truth about some event – so as not to embarrass their country – would conflict with the principle of truth-telling in general.

2   Compatibility with ethical themes

A claim of patriotism should be tested by the three great themes of ethics: the good, the right and the dutiful, and the virtuous.

With regard to the good, we ask about the good or bad consequences of being patriotic to x in situation y by doing z. For example, what are the consequences of patriotically supporting a war? We also ask about the implications of certain *notions* of patriotism. For instance, is it a consequence of your view of patriotism that officials, as patriots, may conceal facts about why a government is going to war? If so, this notion of patriotism justifies the actions of several presidents who lied to Americans about the Vietnam War, as revealed by the publication of the Pentagon Papers in the early 1970s. With regard to rights and duties, does a patriotic claim violate the human rights of citizens; or ask an official to not fulfill a duty? As for virtue, how might the patriotic action affect the moral character of citizens? For instance, does the notion that patriotism means "my country right or wrong" encourage citizens to not deliberate carefully about issues and to be too obedient to government?

3   Compatibility with journalism principles

A claim of patriotism should be compatible with the major principles of democratic journalism, as expressed in codes of ethics, from minimizing harm to reporting the truth without fear or favor. Also, citizens who make patriotic claims must remember that journalists have special democratic roles that must be taken into account. For instance, asking journalists to not question a government's decision to enter a war violates the watchdog function of journalism.

4   Compatibility with democratic patriotism

A claim to patriotism must be compatible with moderate, democratic patriotism. There are five tests:

a   *The claim of patriotism is moderate and democratic:* Is the claim of patriotism a form of extreme or moderate patriotism? What is the object of this patriotism? Is it allegiance to the commands of a charismatic leader, or is it love of democratic society?

b   *The claim of patriotism is inclusive:* It respects the rights and freedoms of all citizens in a nation. Patriotism has no moral force when it supports actions that favor a subsection of citizens or the repression of a subsection of citizens.

c   *The claim of patriotism is restrained:* It is not xenophobic about other peoples. It lacks the aggressiveness associated with robust nationalism and extreme forms of patriotism. The policy must be consistent with fair relations among countries and respect principles of international law and human rights.

d   *The claim of patriotism is evidentially strong:* The claim is supported by strong empirical evidence and logical argument, not merely emotion and group pressure. The evidence includes the aforementioned analysis of consequences. The facts upon which the claim is based must indeed be facts, not convenient myths, stereotypes, and unsubstantiated generalizations.

e   *The claim of patriotism must survive sustained public scrutiny and investigation:* Such evaluation can only be made in a public sphere that is informed by a free press.

By using these tests, journalists erect an ethical barrier against immoderate claims of patriotism. Yet, honoring the standards will require independence and courage. Journalism's democratic values come under severe test when a country decides to go to war, to deny civil liberties for security reasons, or to ignore the constitution in order to quell domestic unrest. The duty of journalists to critique a country's leadership may be very unpopular in times of war. The publication of a government's human and civil rights abuses in a military campaign may lead to accusations that the press is aiding the enemy. In times of uncertainty, journalists have a duty to continue to provide news, investigations, controversial analysis, and multiple perspectives. They should not mute their criticisms, and they should maintain skepticism toward all sources. Journalists need to unearth and explain the roots of their country's problems and assess alleged threats. Journalists need to fact-check and verify patriotic claims like any other important political claim. They need to defend the freedom to question such claims.

Section 2: globalism and patriotism

In defining democratic patriotism, I have done what I can to incorporate the partiality of patriotism into moral reasoning. But it is still not enough. Nation-based patriotism is too parochial to guide journalism in an era of global reporting on global issues. Moreover, we need an additional restraint on patriotism beyond the four-criterion test. Patriotism needs to be compatible with global values such as advancing global democracy, reducing global poverty, and respect for human rights anywhere in the world. And, even more, journalists (and citizens) need to make global values the very foundation of their ethics, and become "global patriots." Journalism ethics should become a global journalism ethics.[12]

The poverty of parochialism

News media today are global in reach and impact, due to technology; but this media can be as parochial, nationalistic, and narrow-minded as the non-global journalism that came before it. Global journalism is not the same thing as a journalism guided by global values.

Why go global? The first reason is that we live in a different world than when media codes were created over a century ago. We live in a world where "reality" is defined and mediated by a ubiquitous and powerful global media. News media are global in content because they report on global issues or events, whether the issue is immigration, climate change, world trade policies, or international security. News media are global in reach because they have the technology to gather information from around the world with incredible speed, and to use this information to create stories for a global public. News media are global in impact because the production of stories has impact across borders, sparking riots in distant lands or prompting global responses to natural disasters. The argument for global journalism ethics can be summarized in one short sentence: global power entails global responsibilities. It is therefore appropriate – and some would say urgent – to ask about the ethics of global media, and to what extent it differs from the previous ethics of a non-global media rooted in individual nations.

The need for a global ethics is due not only to technological innovation and new ownership patterns; it is due to changes in the world that journalism inhabits. Of primary importance is the fact that our media-connected world brings together a plurality of different religions, traditions, ethnic groups, values, and organizations with varying political agendas, social ideals, and conceptions of the good. Media content deemed offensive by certain groups can spark not just domestic unrest but global tension. In such a climate, the role of media, and its ethics, must be re-examined.

A globally minded journalism is of great value because a biased and parochial media can wreak havoc in a tightly linked global world. North American readers may fail to understand the causes of violence in the Middle East or of drought in Africa if they are not reported properly. Jingoistic reports can portray the inhabitants of other regions of the world as a threat. In times of insecurity, a narrow-minded, patriotic news media can amplify the views of leaders who stampede populations into war or the removal of civil rights for minorities. We need a cosmopolitan media that reports issues in a way that reflects this global plurality of views and groups to understand each other better. We also need globally responsible media to help citizens understand the daunting global problems of poverty, immigration, and environmental degradation.

A second reason was noted in Chapter 1: the rise of misinformation and extreme populism in a global public sphere. This extremism plays upon patriotic feelings, using dramatic images and false claims to incite fear, hatred, and nationalism. To counter-balance this trend, journalists need to ground their ethical perspective on global values.

A third reason is that a parochial journalism cannot be entrusted with the vital role of supporting human rights around the world. An ethic that prioritizes parochial interests cannot be the global moral conscience needed to protect and advance human rights. History teaches us that parochialism is an unsteady guide for ethics, especially for international issues. One only has to review the history of the two world wars of the last century, and the horrific Holocaust, to question the moral competency of parochialism in global affairs.

Moreover, it seems today that, at almost every turn, some form of parochialism threatens to weaken our resolve to deal effectively with global issues. Parochialism can erode the will to work according to larger and nobler global principles. People justify their inaction in addressing global poverty and injustice by citing slogans such as "charity begins at home," or they soft-peddle assistance to distressed foreigners as a laudable but optional form of benevolence. Or, hard-nosed realists warn us that, in a world of competing nations, globalism is a soft-headed luxury we cannot afford. For a recent example of distorted media coverage due to strong parochial feelings, consider the coverage in Europe and the United States of the 2015–2016 refugee crises, as thousands fleeing war in Syria and elsewhere sought to reach parts of Europe. In many countries, such as Italy and Greece, journalists became megaphones for groups with their inaccurate facts, xenophobic fears, and proposals that violated human rights treaties.[13]

Parochialism needs to be corrected, limited, and counter-balanced by global principles.

Parochial and global selves

What does it mean to be parochial or global in one's values?

For many of us, our value systems are a mix of global and parochial values. But most of the time, parochialism is our default setting. The original meaning of parochial is what belongs to the parish, what is close to us. Therefore, a parochial value is an attachment to something or someone because it is "near, dear, and familiar." The parochial is, typically, communal, associated with the people, and places of our upbringing. It forms part of our current identity. Parochial values display an extraordinary variety. My parochial values include an attachment to 1960s rock music and the seafaring traditions of Atlantic Canada, where I was born.

Our parochial self includes group parochialism, a love of groups to which I belong or with which I identify. Typically, these groups are my family, my kin, my close friends and colleagues, my ethnic group. It can extend to something as large as my nation, and beyond. People who are not members of my favored groups are outsiders, and my attitude to them may be one of indifference, suspicion, or hostility. Globalization has not extinguished tribalism.

Globalism is a deliberate attempt to develop a value scheme *not* based on parochialism – not based on my attachments to specific things and groups. Globalism finds value in things and in people for reasons other than the fact that they are "mine" or belong to my favored group. The principles of globalism do not derive their normative force from the contingencies of where anyone was born and what groups populate their social environment. Global values apply to all people as people and transcend parochial boundaries.

What values are those? They are things that promote the development and flourishing of the most inclusive group of all: humanity. A globalist cares about humans of all kinds, and their fate, as a whole. This attachment has expressed itself in ethical principles scattered across centuries of religious, ethical, and philosophical thought, not to mention social movements. Take, for example, the value of human rights, i.e., the attribution of rights to people simply because they are human. Globalism is on view in the UN's *Universal Declaration of Human Rights*. Or consider the Christian doctrine that one should love all humans because they are made in the image of God. This idea receives a secular interpretation in Kant's notion of the overwhelming dignity and worth of humans.[14] There is the cosmopolitan principle that all people are moral equals and therefore we have strong duties to strangers.[15] One can detect the global spirit in art, music, and the humanities. In pop music, there is the enduring popularity of John Lennon's *Imagine*; in classical music, there is Beethoven's sublime *Ode to Joy*. We sense the workings of globalism in moral theories that require us to adopt impartial perspectives when dealing with others, or to work for global social justice. Globalism does not ask humans to deny parochial values, but to restrain and transcend them when they conflict with global principles.

The moral quandary of our global world derives from the fact that humans are capable of feeling the force of both parochial and global values, and to be torn between them in many situations. One way to resolve the tension is to make one set of values primary. The tension is a decision whether to adopt one of two moral theses – moral parochialism or moral globalism.

Moral parochialism asserts that it is not only ethically permissible but morally correct to ground one's morality on parochial values. One's first duty is to your country and co-nationals. *Moral globalism* asserts the opposite. It is not only ethically permissible but morally correct to ground one's morality on global values. Which thesis one adopts has far-reaching consequences for political and moral judgments. For instance, parochialists tend to support less foreign aid and humanitarian intervention. The globalist counters that assistance to distressed strangers is a duty prescribed by global principles, so it is not a matter of charity.[16]

Global patriots

Given these two theses, we can distinguish between parochial and global journalism ethics. Parochial journalists make parochial values primary, such as serving their nation, when they define their social role, state their principles, and decide how and what to cover. The moral parochial thesis in journalism is: *the primary duty of a journalist is to support and promote the interests of a group of which the journalist is a member – typically the public of a nation, or the members of a religious or ethnic group.* The global thesis in journalism is: *the primary duty of a journalist is to support and promote the interests of human flourishing at large and to place global values ahead of parochial values.*[17]

To some people, the parochial thesis is obvious. Who could object to journalists serving their nation through informative reports? Since journalism outlets are located in communities, is it not correct for journalists to be parochial, i.e., to serve local publics? But, as noted, patriotic pressures can compromise truth-telling. Can journalists be impartial in reporting *yet* favor their nation when reporting on issues that affect their country, such as trade treaties? There are reasons to "go global" in ethics. I propose that journalists disrupt this norm by becoming global patriots, first; national patriots, second. A global patriot adopts globalism. Journalists see themselves as public communicators to a global public sphere. Global patriotism is loyalty to humanity. If journalists choose globalism, they adopt a global identity expressed by three imperatives:

1   *Act as global agents*: Journalists should see themselves as ethical agents of a global public sphere. The goal of their collective actions is a well-informed global "info-sphere" that challenges the distortions of tyrants, the abuse of human rights, and the manipulation of information by special interests.

2   *Serve the citizens of the world*: The global journalist's primary loyalty is to the information needs of world citizens. Journalists should refuse to define themselves as attached primarily to factions, regions, or even countries.
3   *Promote non-parochial understandings:* The global journalist frames issues broadly and uses a diversity of sources and perspectives to promote a nuanced global understanding of issues.

What would change?

Globalism is not just an ideal. It has practical implications. It requires a sea change in the concepts and practices of journalism ethics.

Consider journalism's social contract. In a global public sphere, journalism has a multi-society contract. The cosmopolitan journalist is a transnational informer who seeks the trust of a global audience. The ideal of objectivity in news coverage goes global. Global journalists do not allow their national bias to distort reports on global issues. The ideas of accuracy and balance also become enlarged to include reports with international sources and cross-cultural perspectives. Global media ethics asks journalists to be more conscious of how they frame major stories, how they set the international news agenda, and how they can spark violence in tense societies. When my country embarks on an unjust war against another country, I, as a journalist (or citizen), should say so. If I am a Canadian journalist and I learn that Canada is engaged in trading practices that condemn citizens of an African country to continuing, abject poverty, I should not hesitate to report the injustice. It is not a violation of patriotism to hold one's country to higher standards.

Making global values primary affects the approach to coverage. Parochial journalists would tend to report a climate change conference from the perspective of their co-patriots: how would a climate treaty serve *our* national interests? Global patriots would cover such events from the perspective of the global public good. What is the global problem concerning climate change and how should all countries cooperative to reach a fair agreement? Global journalists from the West would transcend their parochialism to report the legitimate complaints of developing nations to climate treaty proposals from their country. The same applies to coverage of trade talks. Parochial journalists would tend to focus on the costs and benefits of an agreement on their country. How would a trade agreement open up markets for *their* nation's farmers or oil producers? Global journalists would question a trade proposal if it advances the interests of their nation, while unfairly harming poor nations. Finally, as seen, globalism reduces the role of patriotism. At best, nation-based patriotism is ethically permissible if it does not conflict with global principles.

Global journalism ethics does not entail that news organizations should ignore local issues or regional audiences. It does not mean that every story requires a cosmopolitan attitude. However, there are situations, such as military intervention in a foreign country, climate change, and the establishment of a fair world trading system, where we need to assess actions from a perspective of global justice and reasonableness. What is at issue is a gradual widening of basic editorial attitudes and standards – a widening of journalists' vision of their responsibilities.

Section 3: human flourishing and rights

Globalism, as described, is a highly general stance that advocates for humanity through global values. Can we develop globalism so it is more specific, and therefore informative? Can we say something more concrete about which global values matter the most? Yes, we can. One way is to think of advancing humanity as advancing the human good and then define the human good by examining its components. The human good is not one single type of good, but a composite of goods. Together, these goods allow humans to enjoy flourishing lives. Human flourishing is the human good. I propose that globalism be based on this principle: *all humans are equally valuable moral agents of a single humanity, and all deserve a flourishing life.*

Flourishing means the exercise of one's intellectual, emotional, and other capacities to a high degree in a just and supportive social context. Ideally, flourishing is the fullest expression of human development under favorable conditions. We draw a portrait of a good life, over time, as an integrated composite of goods, and we make this portrait the ultimate aim of action and ethics. In reality, humans flourish in varying degrees. Few people flourish fully. Life often goes badly; many live in desperate conditions where flourishing is a remote ideal. Nevertheless, flourishing helps us to evaluate social systems.

Four levels

To identify the goods that define human flourishing, we think about what humans have in common. What are the common needs to be met and capacities to be developed? These goods are "primary goods" because they allow us to pursue other goods.

Flourishing, I contend, is the development of four levels of primary goods – individual, social, and political goods, and the goods of justice. To achieve the goods of each level is to achieve a corresponding form of human dignity: individual, social, and political dignity, and the dignity of justice.[18] The dignity we seek for citizens in our society, we seek for humanity. Figure 4.1 outlines the four levels.

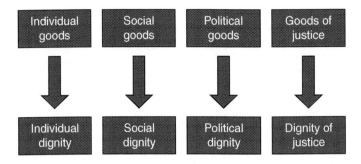

Figure 4.1 Four levels of human flourishing and dignity

By individual goods, I mean the goods that come from the development of each individual's capacities. This level includes the physical goods that allow physical dignity. All persons need food, shelter, and security to live a normal length of life in health. This level also includes the development of our rationality and moral character so that our physical capacities flower into distinct human traits. Such a person has individual dignity, or the dignity of a person. The social goods arise from participation in society: the freedom to enter into economic associations, the goods of love and friendship; the need for mutual recognition and respect. In this manner, we achieve social dignity. By political goods, I mean the goods of living in egalitarian democracy. These goods include the basic liberties, such as freedom of speech, combined with the opportunity and resources to exercise these freedoms. A citizen who enjoys these goods has political dignity, through self-government.

By the goods of justice, I mean the goods that come from living among persons and institutions of ethical character. To flourish, we need to live among people who are disposed to be what Rawls calls morally "reasonable."[19] In developing our core capacities on all four levels, the goods of justice are especially important. We should pursue our goods *within* the bounds of justice. We should not enlarge our goods at the expense of others.

Journalism and the four levels

Journalists, as global patriots, seek the four dignities for humanity. How?

Individual goods

1   monitor basic levels of individual dignity. Does society provide a
     decent level of physical goods such as food, shelter, health, wealth, a

reasonable length of life, and physical security? How effective is the educational system? Do citizens have an opportunity to learn about and engage in scientific and cultural trends?

2   investigate inequality. Journalists should publish investigations into those who have been denied goods, and then pressure institutions to address inequalities. Reveal whether gender, ethnicity, or other differences account for inequalities. By exploring below the surface of society, journalists show who "equal" their egalitarian society really is.

Social goods

1   report critically on economic associations. Does society allow all citizens to participate in the economy, and how does society distribute economic power?

2   assess the quality of social life. Journalism should report on social and technological trends, and whether the trends nurture collective activity, and flourishing communities.

3   assist social bridging. In a pluralistic world, journalism has a duty to act as a bridge between classes, ethnic groups, religions, and cultures within and among countries.

4   assist media literacy and the evaluation of media: journalism should examine the impact of media on society and how communication technology can assist minorities.

5   use global comparisons. Journalists should evaluate the levels of human good among countries and report on different approaches to social problems.

Political goods

1   critique the basic structure. Encourage deliberation on issues of justice, and investigate the performance of institutions of justice.

2   monitor basic liberties. Defend liberties around the world. To what extent do citizens enjoy the full value of liberties, such as freedom from discrimination? Are citizens able to exercise these freedoms for the purpose of self-development?

3   encourage participation and diverse representation in media.

Goods of justice

1   critique people and policies that claim to be motivated by the public good. In reality, who wins or loses? Cover individuals and groups who truly enhance the public good.

2   support public reason through dialogic media: create dialogic spaces.

Journalism and human rights

A concern with human rights should be central to a global ethic.[20]

How has Western journalism ethics treated rights? Again, parochialism has been the master norm. Political and human rights *within* a nation have received the greatest attention, especially the liberties of the press and the liberties of the public. Press philosophy in the 1700s, for example, argued that journalists served the Enlightenment public in return for constitutional guarantees of freedom of the press. In the mid-1800s, a liberal democratic view portrayed journalists as watchdogs on the rights of co-nationals. In the 20th century, the press expanded its notion of rights to include issues of equality within its national boundaries, such as a woman's right to vote and the right of American blacks to attend non-segregated schools.

What conception of human rights is appropriate for global journalism ethics? Boylan divides theories of human rights according to how they justify human rights claims.[21] He notes three kinds: (1) theories that justify human rights legally and contractually, e.g., there are laws that endorse human rights. (2) Theories that justify human rights as promoting the basic interests and welfare of people. (3) Theories that justify human rights as providing the freedom and autonomy that people need to become self-directed agents, and to develop their capacities.

My view of human rights stems from my view of ethics, what I call contractual naturalism.[22] The social force of ethical norms is due to an agreement on rules of social cooperation, as stated in Chapter 3. Norms signal agreement on the value of certain goods, freedoms, pleasures, and what makes us happy or productive. All of these "things" are part of human nature and our place in the natural world. The ground of ethics is nothing more, and nothing less, than what reasonable people, reviewing their experience and listening to others, believe should be the rule.

I define a right as an ethical claim that certain freedoms to develop capacities and engage in certain activities are so important to human flourishing that it would be wrong for anyone to deny such activity. Society has a duty to respect rights, such as the right to educated oneself and the right to not be subjected to torture. Human rights are among the most fundamental of all our rights. They are what we consider necessary for the flourishing of all human beings.

Globalism in journalism, therefore, is committed to the support and protection of human rights and part of the duty to advocate for human flourishing.

Conclusion: ultimate aims

With this notion of human rights, we can now articulate a full statement of the aims of democratically engaged journalism.

Democratically engaged journalists, in adopting the stance of a global patriot, make their primary duty the promotion of human flourishing and, as a crucial component of flourishing, (1) the protection of human rights and (2) the strengthening of egalitarian democratic culture and institutions globally.

Notes

1 See Ward, *Invention of Journalism Ethics*, 224–226.
2 Nussbaum, "Patriotism and Cosmopolitanism."
3 Tolstoy, *Writings on Civil Disobedience and Nonviolence*, 142.
4 However, see *Handbook of Patriotism*, ed. Mitja Sardoc.
5 Nathanson, *Patriotism, Morality, and Peace*, 12.
6 Nussbaum, *Political Emotions*, 2, 208.
7 See Viroli, *For Love of Country*.
8 Viroli, *For Love of Country*, 169.
9 Nathanson, *Patriotism, Morality and Peace*, 37–38.
10 Ortega y Gasset, *Meditations on Quixote*, 105.
11 The phrase "blood and belonging" is from Ignatieff, *Blood and Belonging*.
12 See Ward, *Global Journalism Ethics*.
13 On media coverage of the refuge crisis, see a study by the Ethical Journalism Network at http://ethicaljournalismnetwork.org/en/contents/moving-stories-international-review-of-how-media-cover-migration.
14 Kant, *Groundwork of the Metaphysics of Morals*, 42–43.
15 See Appiah, *Cosmopolitanism: Ethics in a World of Strangers*.
16 See my "The Moral Priority of Globalism in a Digital World."
17 See "The Moral Priority of Globalism in a Digital World."
18 On the human good, see my *Global Journalism Ethics*, Chapters 3 and 5.
19 Rawls, *Political Liberalism*, 48.
20 On human rights, see Hayden, *The Philosophy of Human Rights*, Boersema, *Philosophy of Human Rights*, and Goodale and Merry, *The Practice of Human Rights*.
21 Boylan, *Natural Human Rights: A Theory*.
22 Contractualism views morality as based on an agreement among members of a society. Naturalism explains morality by appeal to only natural capacities, without appeal to deities or non-natural forces. See Darwall, *Contractarianism/ Contractualism*, and Sayre-McCord, "Contractarianism."

5   Disrupt the public
sphere – detox

Before completing this book, I promote disruption in two other areas of journalism. One is to disrupt the public sphere, the subject of this chapter. The second is to disrupt how we think about the field of journalism ethics, the topic of the final chapter.

In Chapter 1, I claimed that we communicate in a polluted public sphere of extreme populists and others who specialize in the dark arts of propaganda, fake news, and intolerant attacks on minorities. Then, in the next three chapters, I have made a case for democratically engaged journalism, as an alternate model of journalism. I now consider practical measures and guidelines for engaged journalism in problem areas.

In this chapter, I consider measures to help detox the public sphere: how to respond to fake news, how to respond to extreme populists, and how journalist and civic groups can collaborate to "macro-resist" these dark arts.[1] My slogan is: *disrupt, invent, and collaborate.*

Section 1: resist fake news

What can journalists do to resist the misinformation that has come to be called fake news? One might think the answer is simple: mainstream journalists can resist fake news by telling the truth and reporting the facts. But this answer mistakenly suggests that fake stories are produced only by the mainstream news media. While it would be difficult to quantify, it is obvious that much of the fake news is produced by political leaders and their ideological supporters, plus other malevolent creators of media content. Also, this answer misleadingly portrays the journalistic quest for truth and fact as a simple matter. As I have discussed earlier, determining what is a fact or what is true is a complex, fallible process. The world does not deliver daily to the door of newsrooms, ready for publication, neat bundles of things called "simple truths" and "simple facts." Instead, journalists ask: what truth? Whose truth? How much truth? Since the origin of modern journalism, journalists have struggled with ascertaining fact and truth for reasons internal and external to the practice. Journalists may lack the specialized knowledge necessary to cover a complex topic. They labor under deadlines, powerful publishers, and finite newsroom resources. Their investigations begin with a jumble of unconfirmed reports from which good journalists ferret out the most plausible account through a gradual accumulation of verified claims. Journalists face a dizzying abundance of interpretations of fact. Many stories deal with matters where no consensus exists and where controversy, bias, and conflict surround the issues. That truth in journalism is a work-in-progress is evident to foreign reporters. In conflict zones, the fog of war severely hampers journalists' search for truth.

Now, on top of all of these obstacles, journalists face the fake news phenomenon of modern global media.

When is news fake?

Fake news can have three meanings. (1) *Unintentional falsehood*: a story, or a part of a story, is false because the journalist makes errors for any number of reasons, such as misunderstanding a set of numbers. (2) *Intentional falsehood*: a journalist intentionally reports falsehoods or misleading descriptions of some event. A journalist may spin the facts or fabricate sources to make the story more sensational than it is. Or, a journalist may report negatively about someone because she dislikes him. (3) *Intentional political falsehood*: a journalist may report falsehoods intentionally for political reasons. The journalist supports an ideology by maligning other views, or publishing badly sourced stories (or rumors) that damage opponents. This is the primary sense in which fake news is used today.

Journalism that makes honest mistakes is not fake news, since "fake" means intentionally produced. The second sense, that journalists intentionally report inaccurately, is nothing new. Fake news is defined by a distinct claim: that the news is intentionally false for political reasons, i.e., the journalist's political bias. President Trump and his supporters dismiss reports as fake news because it is the work of "liberal media" that allegedly work to undermine their agenda.[2]

The idea of fake news, as politically inspired stories, is so general that it is easily misused by members of the left or right wing, although it appears to be more popular these days among the right wing. The charge of fake news becomes weaponized to "knock down" any report that is unfavorable to one's political ideology. You can make a fake news charge, without caring about the facts. You simply claim that the report is politically motivated. Strangely, the charge of fake news becomes one more piece of fake news.

So the first thing that journalists can do is to *not* use the term "fake news" unless necessary. And, if they must, use it cautiously and explain the context, e.g., report that it was the prime minister who called the story fake news, he does so frequently, and he did not justify the claim with specific facts. If a leader uses the term too liberally, journalists should challenge him to say exactly what is wrong with a report. The only possible cure for the weaponization of a term is to push back against its use.

Also, journalists and others can resist fake news by strengthening their fact-checking procedures, letting citizens know if a statement is a fact, almost a fact, or a "pants on fire" lie. Fact-checking is already a major "industry" as dozens of newsrooms and civic groups fact-check election campaigns, statements by presidents, and so on. For example, at Harvard, the Shorenstein Center announced that First Draft, a coalition against fake news, is moving into the center. First Draft has helped coalitions fact-check elections in France and elsewhere.[3] Given the proliferation of fact checkers, citizens should be careful about which checkers they consult.

By itself, fact-checking is inadequate. Why? Because, as stated in Chapter 3, the public needs so many other things from media than the checking of specific factual claims. It needs informed analysis, deep explanatory journalism, and journalists skilled in the interpretation of complex trends. We need to know more than that a politician made a false statement. We need to challenge questionable policy and the misinterpretation of political principles. Journalism should remind citizens about the very conditions of plural democracy, such as the value of tolerance, equality, minority rights, the separation of powers, and so on. These are crucial social and philosophical understandings that are skewed and simplified in the media.

Moreover, fact-checking presumes most citizens are open to *all* of the facts. But, what if many citizens, say in the United States, are so ideologically divided that they will not listen to facts? Or they listen only to facts that suit their views and originate from like-minded news outlets? What if, tomorrow, the *New York Times* published true stories of importance about the Trump presidency and a substantial number of Americans ignored it because it was issued by "liberal" media? Here, the problem is larger than revealing false facts.

So what else can be done?

Objective stance in journalism

Journalists should employ a method of evaluation that includes not only checking facts but also the checking theories, historical viewpoints and interpretations of law, rights, and political principles. Such a method, in broad outline, exists. In Chapter 2, I proposed the method of holistic objectivity as a method for testing almost any type of statement. I said holistic objectivity consisted of an objective stance and the testing of interpretations by two types of standard – generic standards of rationality and standards specific to the practice in question. I now want to say how that method would work in journalism.

Journalists adopt the objective stance by displaying a number of cognitive virtues – dispositions that help inquiry. They define the mindset that helps us to know the world in as rigorous a manner as possible, reducing the influence of bias. The main virtues are four in number: *open rationality, partial transcendence, a desire for disinterested truth, and integrity.*

Objective journalists practice open rationality in their domain of inquiry by accepting the aforementioned burdens of rationality – to listen to all sides, to learn from criticism, and to be accountable to the public for the content of their reports. Objective journalists exhibit partial transcendence by putting aside, at least temporarily, their biases and parochial preferences. They put a critical distance between themselves and approach stories with a healthy skepticism. The objective journalist is disposed towards disinterested truth if he or she refuses to prejudge a story and follows the facts to the truth, wherever the facts lead. The disinterested journalist does not allow personal interests to overwhelm the passion for truth. She is willing to correct errors. She is willing to admit that a story idea is wrong-headed. By following these and other virtues, the objective journalist acts with integrity.

Standards of evaluation

But, as noted in Chapter 2, adopting the objective stance is not sufficient. Objective journalists must put these virtues to work by applying the two levels of evaluative standards to stories. On the first level, of generic standards, they should base any report on sufficient evidence derived from reliable observations and, where possible, from solid empirical studies. A report should not contain logical inconsistencies, manipulative rhetoric, or fallacies. If claims violate well-known facts and established knowledge, the journalist investigates this incoherence.

Pragmatic objectivity also requires reports to satisfy standards specific to journalism. There are five types of standard.

1   *standards of empirical validity:* Accuracy, verification, and completeness are prime empirical standards in journalism. Accuracy calls for accurate quotations and paraphrases of statements and correct numbers. It forbids manipulation of news images and use of misleading dramatizations and "reconstructions" of events. It asks: what is the

empirical evidence for the story? Are the facts carefully collected? Are counter-facts treated seriously? Verification calls on reporters to cross-check claims of potential whistleblowers against original documents. The standard of completeness means that stories should be substantially complete by including the essential facts, main consequences, and major viewpoints.

2   *standards of clarity, logic, and coherence:* Beyond the checking of facts, holistic objectivity requires additional tests. Does the story cohere with existing knowledge in the field? Is the newsmaker's interpretation logically consistent? Are their concepts clear? Are fallacious arguments or manipulative techniques used? Codes of ethics for journalism typically do not spell out standards of coherence. They do not contain directives to "be logical" or "test your claim against other beliefs." But quality journalism tests for coherence at every turn. Any journalist who has tried to construct a complex story knows that the coherence of evidence from many sources is a prime consideration. Any journalist who has tried to report on an alleged scientific breakthrough knows how important it is to evaluate the claim by comparing it with existing scientific knowledge.

3   *standards of diverse and trusted sources:* Journalists need to make sure their sources are diverse and reliable, and, if they claim to be experts, they are truly experts in their field as judged by their work. Journalists need sources drawn only from elite institutions but include ordinary people, minorities, and the people who are most affected by some event. This is not the idea of a quantitative balance, where two rival spokespersons are quoted in equal length. It is "appropriate diversity" which differs depending on the story. For example, equal balance does not apply to all stories. There is no need to quote someone who favors sex with children to report on child sex abuse in an orphanage. The aim is to represent the views of all relevant groups.

4   *standards of self-consciousness:* Journalists need to reflect on themselves. In constructing a story, are they conscious of the frame they use to understand the topic? Are there other frames? What are the assumptions they make in approaching the story in this manner? What is their role in reporting this event? Does their use of language reflect a bias?

5   *standards of open, public scrutiny:* Have journalists subjected their opinions to the views of others? Are they prepared to alter our views?

In summary, a report is objective to the degree that it derives from an objective stance and satisfies these generic and domain-specific standards. The standards apply to many forms of journalism from "straight" reporting to editorial commentary and advocacy journalism. It is a flexible, platform-neutral method.

Pragmatic objectivity is a powerful tool for combatting biased reporting and fake news, whether the story is done by a mainstream journalist or a manipulative political agent. Most fake news will be identified if one applies the method rigorously. Reports will not be "politically inspired reports" if journalists adopt the objective stance and apply its standards to themselves. There is no better antidote to fake news than real news, objectively tested.

Section 2: resist extremism

In today's media ecology, journalists need to develop methods for dealing with extremists who claim to be populists and use extreme (or hate) speech. Extremism creates its own problems for journalists. While extremists circulate fake news, their messages are not just intentionally false. They are extreme and may incite violence against vulnerable groups.

By extreme speech, I mean statements that ridicule and demean groups, violating the norms of moderate, egalitarian democracy defined in Chapter 3. Often, the messages are racist, targeting Jews, Muslims, and new immigrants as lazy, dangerous or less than human – inferior in intelligence and moral character. The list of such groups and leaders includes: Marine Le Pen of the National Front in France, Geert Wilders in the Netherlands, former far-right Austrian politician Jörg Haider of the Alliance for the Future of Austria, and Brexit promoter Nigel Farage in Britain. These leaders speak for groups that no longer lack popular support. In Germany, President Angela Merkel has struggled to contain right wing groups, such as Alternative for Germany, which use the immigration crisis to sow popular dissent. In Italy, the far-right Five Star Movement attracted a large share of the vote in the 2018 Italian election.

Once on the fringes of mainstream politics, these groups recruit members and gain popular support by portraying themselves as populists who are the true friends of "the people" because they fight corrupt elites in government. They gather support by instilling fear and tribalism into the public sphere. This extreme populism is anything but an egalitarian form of populism that promotes the participation of all groups in society, equally. For extreme populists, "the people" is actually a sub-set of the populace – those groups they favor and treat as superior. Extreme populism is based on the anti-democratic, anti-egalitarian idea of the alleged *rightful dominance of a certain group of citizens, which comes to define the people.*

Guidelines for extreme populism

What guidelines can help journalists to develop practices for covering extremists who claim they are populists? Here are some ideas:

Know your populism

Define populism carefully: Help citizens know the core ideas of populism. Be capable of defining extreme populism and recognizing
examples of undemocratic demagoguery. Challenge the extreme
populist's strategies to protect democracy.

Know your history: Know how populism arose in your culture and
how it can take many forms. Do not define it as always a negative
phenomenon.

Be specific and critical

Use populist language carefully: Do not over-use populist language; do
not call anyone who appeals to the public, or claims to be an outsider
against the establishment, a "populist."

*Be specific when you question people and movements who claim to
be populist:* Demand that populists explain their meaning of "populism" and what they think it entails for public policy. Question their
claim to be populist.

Cover extreme populists where necessary, but carefully

There will be circumstances where coverage is required, e.g., an extremist
gains significant support in an election. Ignoring such developments will
only give rise to the charge of an elite media censoring free speech, and
may even create public support for the leader. Yet, coverage must provide
deep, contextual information about these leaders and their views. Without
context, audiences may regard the extreme populist as novel, provocative
(in a stimulating way), and not that harmful. Extreme populist ideas should
not be simply repeated, where the reporter, seeking neutrality, becomes a
mouthpiece for extreme claims.

Do not be baited

Don't overreact to "elite" criticism: Extreme populists will seek to
characterize journalists as untrustworthy elites writing fake news.
Resist becoming entangled in that debate. Perhaps the only thing to
do is for media outlets to be transparent about their ownership, their
political perspectives, and editorial processes – and the firm factual
basis for their reports.

Meet the populist on the high ground of ideas: Few people will win
a name-calling dispute with an extreme populist. They are skilled
at innuendo, stereotypes, and feeding the biases of their audiences.

Journalists should not use the same demeaning forms of argumentation. Journalists need to challenge the extreme populist's ideas – will their idea *really* resolve a problem? What is the evidence for this claim?

Stay calm and keep your powder dry: Journalists should not allow themselves to be "baited" into responding publicly in a manner that reinforces the extreme populist's negative view of media. For example, at a news conference, if Trump or some other leader makes fun of a journalist's question, or personally attacks the journalist as biased or stupid, do not reply in the same manner. Maintain your cool, and keep asking factual questions (despite the in-coming verbal "flak"), or keep referring to your facts. Let your research do the talking.

Advance egalitarian democracy

As noted in previous chapters, journalists should advance democratic dialogue across racial, ethnic, and economic divisions. They should go deep politically.

Meanwhile, what about the *content* of the extremist's speech? What if they use extreme speech at public meetings and in public statements? Here are more ideas:

Testing speech

Area 1: who is the speaker or actor?

Journalists should consider the credibility of sources when reporting an event. Even more so when they cover strong statements that affect relations among groups: reports should include information on the speakers and their backgrounds.

- Who is the speaker, and what is their political biography? Has the person been associated with groups that have expressed bigoted or extreme views? What has this person said and done in the past? How credible and reliable has he been? Has he ever suggested (or clearly advocated) discriminatory or violent actions?
- Does the speaker's statement show a pattern of extreme speech and discriminatory language, or was his strong statement a one-time, emotional reaction? If it is a "one – time" reaction, will the speaker be willing to retract or moderate their statement?
- How media-savvy, powerful, and manipulative is the speaker?

Area 2: what is the aim of the speech?

By considering the statements and context, seek to determine:

- Is the primary (or only) aim of the speech to demean others and attack the rights and dignity of certain groups? Is the aim to stir up racist or other passions in a tense setting? If the aim is primarily to stir hatreds, and the speaker is not influential or reliable, journalists should consider not covering the event.
- Are other aims present, such as recruiting followers or pressuring government to enact certain policies, such as restricting immigrants?

Area 3: affiliation and sources of support

Journalists should report on the speaker's group:

- What is the group's history, aims, and attitude toward other groups?
- Why is this event occurring, here and now?
- What are the group's financial and political sources of support?
- What is their political significance? For example, in polls and elections, what level of public support do they receive? What level of coverage is justified?

Area 4: content of statements and coverage

What are the content and style of the speech?

- What degree of extremism is indicated by what is stated? Consider the forms of expression, e.g., dehumanizing a group by comparing members to an insect or mocking a group with nicknames and racial slurs.
- What content from the event should go into the reports? Should reports use racist or inaccurate representations of a group? Should reports use offensive gestures or symbols that could inflame community tensions? Should one report that offensive remarks were made but avoid direct quotations?
- How much media "play" does the story warrant; what prominence should it have on the newscast, in the newspaper, or on the news web site? How often will the images and audio of the event be repeated? How can you maintain proportionality in coverage?
- Should the news outlet explain why and how they reported the event and refer to the outlet's editorial guidelines?

Area 5: testing of facts and for evidence

For stories on hate speech, journalists incur an extra duty to test dubious claims and question any allegedly "scientific" studies cited. Fact-check vigorously.

- Does the report asses the alleged facts cited by the newsmaker, such as numbers that would exaggerate a problem?
- Do journalists seek out independent experts to analyze or rebut claims?
- Be aware of techniques familiar to propaganda and hate speech, such as the use of emotional language and name calling, scape-goating, and stereotyping.
- If an extreme group increases its popular support in polls, journalists should maintain a critical, vigilant stance. They should not let down their critical "guard" to appear neutral.

Area 6: consequences for political culture

To promote a tolerant society, journalists should ask these questions:

- What will be the impact of this story, and stories like it, on the groups maligned, and how they are represented in society? Will the stories increase the likelihood of discrimination or violence, or the denial of social dignity?
- Will such stories help to undermine the norms of reasonable political culture and negate a willingness to cooperate and dialogue?
- Has the journalist considered ways of minimizing harm by not publishing highly inflammatory statements or images?
- Are the groups attacked or misrepresented given an opportunity to reply to the claims?

These guidelines show how much *new* work needs to be done in journalism ethics.

Section 3: macro-resistance

So far, I have discussed the problems in a manner that calls for responses from individual journalists and individual news organizations. That is only half of the story. Detoxing the public sphere will require collaboration among many players in government, civil society, and media.

I call this collaboration "macro-resistance" – a global collaboration of diverse organizations and publics who are concerned about their media and their world. Only macro-resistance can counter macro-corruption. It is time to create, at the center of our media system, a networked core of groups that care about responsible communication for a democratic community. We need to *connect* across many boundaries. Journalists, scientists, librarians, data workers, community advocates, and others need to join in macroresistance to fakery, harassment, ideology, and manipulation.

Here are some ways to collaborate.

Global coalition for accountability

Journalists, with academics and media foundations, should build national coalitions for media accountability in their countries and, then, knit them together into a global coalition, with globalism as its ethical base.

In each country, I envisage a system of online, networked centers, independent of government or any one media organization, and plural – open to many approaches to media. Universities, journalism organizations, media ethicists, NGOs, media web sites, news councils, and citizens would create a high-quality resource for daily media discourse, evaluation, and promotion of excellence.

The coalition's functions would include fact-checking, exposure of dubious sources, debate on media ethics and the coverage of events, and the development of new ethical norms for global journalism. Crucial to the coalition(s) is that it be *high-profile* – well-known to the public as a trusted place to check a media source and debate media policy. The hub of this network could be a major school of journalism or, for example, a multi-disciplinary center for democracy. Whatever its structure, it would be a place for macro-resistance, a center of gravity amid the information wars that engulf us.

Building the coalition would take imagination, leadership, and resources. Turf wars will flare. But there *are* resources out there. In North America, the Association for Education in Journalism and Mass Communication has thousands of members – instructors and students of media at dozens of universities and colleges. There are numerous journalism societies and media foundations, and many civil society groups concerned about information. Their macro-resistance would be greater if they joined in common cause.

Creating a sixth estate

The coalition would be a major step toward the creation of a society-wide sixth estate that would focus on evaluating the media practice not only of mainstream journalists but also the media practice of citizens and advocacy groups. Much has been written about the "fifth estate" – online critics of mainstream news media. For several decades, bloggers and online commentators have skewered the mainstream news media for ethical lapses.

Now it is time for citizens and journalists online and offline to create a daily critique of potentially anyone who publishes journalistic material online. We need to expose the limitations, inaccuracies, and attachments of any media worker, anywhere. We need a daily aggregate of both good and bad ethical practice online, and we need to publicly name and shame those who refuse to be accountable for the harm they cause others. Also, the sixth estate can support efforts to create a new media ethics that will outline our digital responsibilities as citizens or journalists.

Understanding "digital reliance"

Macro-resistance requires a better understanding of why citizens rely on, or trust, some media sources more than others. To reach a deeper knowledge in this area, collaboration between journalists and academics is important. Journalists should share with academics the methods they use to monitor audience confidence in their work and allow academics to test these methods relative to other ideas on building reliance in digital news media. Journalists should also test the new hypotheses of academics on media use and reliance.

We need to disrupt the language of media trust, and replace it with the concept of citizen *reliance* on digital media. I believe that most polls on public confidence in news media are measuring the wrong thing – trust. Trust should be reserved for one's partner, spouse, close friends, and colleagues. Trust is personal and intense. I don't think our relations with media and other impersonal institutions amount to trust.[4] Further, I don't think we should trust any institution. We should grant them a temporary and earned credibility. We should try to understand and measure what I call "digital reliance" – how people come to rely on certain media as more reliable than others. The public has a right to rely on journalists to provide accurate reports. Journalism must earn the public's reliance every day. The judgment that media sources are worthy of our reliance is tentative, fallible, and dependent on performance over time.

Relying on media no longer consists in trusting what one news anchor or one newspaper tells us. This is a passive, top-down form of trusting. Today, media evaluation is active and plural, as we compare stories from many sources and we share stories among us. Today, media evaluation is active and plural, as we compare stories from many sources and we share stories among us. We need a digital *epistemology* of media reliance grounded in actual media use.[5]

Ethics literacy

Macro-resistance will falter unless journalists, educators, and citizens combine to make journalism ethics a more inclusive, socially central, enterprise than ever before. They need to dispense with the traditional view of journalism ethics as the debating of decisions in newsrooms, or the modifying of codes of ethics within newsrooms by editors.

In a world where citizens create media content and participate in news coverage, journalism ethics becomes part of a broader media ethics – the norms of using any kind of media. We need a *media ethics for everyone*, a broad communication ethics that addresses cyber bullying and other issues beyond journalism. We need to start teaching media and ethics literacy early in public education. Media literacy tends to be non-normative, examining facts about news media, such as who owns the media, how content is produced, and how to evaluate online data. Ethics literacy builds upon this empirical knowledge by studying the norms of responsible media usage and using these norms to critique media producers of all kinds.

Educators should design curricula for teaching media and ethics literacy, perhaps developing an international template sponsored by the United Nations. In universities, we should teach media and journalism ethics across faculties, not just in journalism schools. We should end the segregation of journalism ethics in schools of journalism and, within the journalism schools, end the further segregation of ethics into one course in the program.

Public-participatory ethics

"Media ethics for everyone" disrupts the way we formulate the questions of journalism ethics, especially when reform of norms in in the air. Journalists tend to think the main questions are: what are the norms that *we* should identify and follow to respond to new ethical problems. Then, typically, news organizations, using committees populated mainly by staff and perhaps a media ethicist, set off to revise their editorial policies and ethical guidelines.

This approach comes from what I and Wasserman have called the era of "closed" professional ethics, contrasted with today's "open" ethics.[6] This is the idea that journalism ethics *belongs* to professional journalists working for mainstream news outlets. Journalism ethics was created by and for professional journalists, and it should stay that way. Professional journalists should control what norms they follow, and control the process of changing norms. A significant number of journalists think that the public can be given a secondary (or supplementary) role, e.g., the public is asked to provide feedback to revised codes. There is also the arrogant view that citizens are not capable of participating in journalism ethics because what do they know about daily journalism?[7]

But what if we look at journalism ethics the other way around? That is, start from the public and ask: what, ethically speaking, do citizens expect, ethically, from their journalists? What new practices and norms would the public support? In Chapter 3, I outlined the public's informational needs from the media. That would be a place to start, when looking at ethics from the public's perspective. Code revisers should give members of the public a meaningful, influential place in articulating and approving ethical practices for news outlets, journalism associations, and so on. This can occur in two ways. First, ethics committees contain several members of the public who play leadings roles in the work of the committees. Second, using social media and other technology, the public can follow the project as it moves long, transparently. The public is also consulted regularly on revisions and their input is seriously taken and incorporated into discussions.

We need a public revolution in *how* we do journalism ethics – the participation of publics in the formulation of standards and in the monitoring of media performance. Rather than talk of media "self-regulation" we should think about a public-participatory ethics – regulation by journalists and citizens, conjointly. Today, an internal, closed approach to ethics is no longer viable. Journalism ethics is "open" – debated and practiced far beyond the confines of mainstream newsrooms. A closed approach only confirms the skepticism of the public that journalists are not willing to be transparent about their ethics and therefore not to be trusted. Public-participatory ethics, in contrast, builds ethics literacy while increasing public confidence in quality journalism. It encourages transparency and accountability of media.

Traditionally, accountability has meant the articulation of journalistic values, procedures to deal with conflicts of interest, accessible methods for public queries, explanations of controversial decisions, firm correction policies with unstinting apologies, and corrective action – showing how the problem will be avoided in the future. Accountability includes press councils and newsroom ombudsmen to respond to readers' complaints. All of these devices of accountability could use improvement. For example, Reuters has improved the transparency of its editorial process with its recently introduced "Backstory" feature which explains the genesis of stories.[8] However, in other areas, there is slow progress. For example, in North America, news councils and ombudsmen (or readers' representatives) who deal with public complaints, are few in number, and relatively unknown to the public.[9] Again, the way that many councils and ombudsmen operate is drawn from an earlier "closed" era. The public does not play a significant and on-going role in the council's work. Moreover, the role of the councils and the ombudsmen are defined in a manner that is limited and "negative" (or complaint-based). Councils have tended to wait for someone to complain about a specific story. I do not want such complaint-resolution mechanisms eliminated. Rather, I would like the agencies to adopt a wider, pro-active stance, such as following the idea of public-participatory ethics. Why not place the materials surrounding any complaint online and encourage the public to comment or judge *before* the council hands down its decision? Also, what if we imagined these agencies as ethics educators at large, in at least two ways. One, go beyond limiting oneself to specific cases. Expand one's analysis to analyze cases *of this sort*, and major trends. Then propose new norms. Also, they could co-sponsor major studies on the ethical health of news media, and hold regular public "town halls" meetings on media ethics? Two, such agents could collaborate with educators and the aforementioned national coalitions to teach "media ethics for everyone," including holding ethics workshops in schools and universities.

At the same time, it is the responsibility of citizens who regularly publish media content to improve *their* accountability. Citizens should adopt, where relevant, the mechanisms of accountability already created by mainstream professional journalism. If you are communicating with the public, you – whomever *you* are – owe concrete and effective accountability methods to your audience.

Collaborating journalists

Meanwhile, how do news outlets find the resources to do important journalism in an era of shrinking budgets? In the USA alone, newsrooms over the past several years have lost at least 28,000 jobs. One response is collaboration among journalists on big stories. The best-known example is the Panama Papers project where hundreds of journalists worked on offshore financing. A recent example of collaboration in Canada was an investigation into the harmful effects of hydrogen sulphide leaking from shale oil wells across Saskatchewan. The investigation discovered oil company violations and dangerous air quality levels kept secret by government. It was conducted by three rival news outlets, such as the *Toronto Star*, and four journalism schools.[10]

Journalism collaboration, increasingly, means collaborating with citizens and civic societies to do engaged forms of local, community reporting – journalism that is not only *about* community but comes *out* of community. The media not only informs the public; it also works toward engaging citizens and creating public debate. Engaged journalism treats audiences as participants. Journalists immerse themselves in communities and listen to how citizens define the issues, while giving the latter a voice in the stories. It could be a radio series on Spaniards who suffer from hunger, or an in-depth look at a homeless camp in Honolulu.[11] For example, engagement with community is the defining concept of the new Agora Center for Journalism at the University of Oregon in the USA. Also, investigative journalists and non-profit news sites are forming global networks to share knowledge of how to mount investigations and to share resources to look at issues in multiple countries.[12] In Canada, there is *Discourse Media*, a Vancouver newsroom that does public journalism funded by citizens, not the state.

Yet with collaboration and partnerships come ethical issues. How do journalists report independently while immersing themselves in community? How do non-profit investigative newsrooms report independently if their funding comes from one or two philanthropic groups? Ethical concerns surround the decision by governments and media organizations, such as Google and Facebook, to fund journalism schools and media literacy education. For example, the University of Arizona's Cronkite Journalism School is partnering with Facebook to study ways for people to engage the news. The Ryerson Journalism School in Toronto recently accepted Facebook funds to launch an "incubator" for new ideas on digital journalism and engaging audiences. Meanwhile, Google Canada is working with civic and government partners to invest $500,000 to teach five million elementary and high school students to be news literate.

While the partnerships appear benevolent and the funding is needed badly, ethical concerns about the independence of journalism instruction, research, and publication should not be dismissed. Agreements to partner need explicit conflict-of-interest clauses, and such measures should be made public. We should not be naïve: Google, Facebook – the "press barons" of today – are not doing this simply out of the goodness of their hearts.

Beyond journalism: society's responsibilities

Neither individual citizens nor professional journalists can detox the public sphere. For citizens, there is no individualistic, technological fix to the problem of macro-pollution, e.g., to simply download a better anti-virus software. Government and society must take steps to address problems beyond what journalists can fix. Macro-resistance requires action from society in general. Technology experts need to protect electoral systems from hacks; our education system needs to prepare digital citizens. Governments can pressure social media to identify fake news, refuse accounts to racists, and be transparent about who pays for ads.

Many of the problems of our polluted public sphere are due to economic and other inequalities between social classes. The issue is how to deal with the differences among us, how to reduce the attraction of fierce ideologies. Journalists can help by being a bridge of understanding among groups, by resisting fake and extreme speech, and by collaborating with others in society. But, here, the problem is larger than journalism. We need economic and social policies that reduce glaring inequalities. We need broad social initiatives to address media literacy and to reduce ideology and hatred. And, citizens have responsibilities to support good media, and adopt good media practices. They should expose themselves online to many viewpoints.[13]

Notes

1 Some of the ideas in sections on journalism objectivity and extremism can be found in my earlier work but appear here with modifications and additions. See *The Invention of Journalism Ethics* and *Ethical Journalism in a Populist Age.*

2 I believe my view of fake news is consistent, in large part, with the view of Brian McNair in his *Fake News*, another book in this Routledge series. Like McNair, I think that fakes news is both new and not new and must be viewed from a wide historical and cultural perspective, including what he identifies as the "crisis of objectivity."

3 See https://shorensteincenter.org/first-draft-joins-shorenstein-center/.

4 See my "Digital Reliance: Public Confidence in Media in a Digital Era."

5 Studies are already underway, e.g. at the University of Missouri www.rjionline.org/reporthtml.html and at the Markkula Center for Applied Ethics https://thetrustproject.org.

6 Ward and Wasserman, "Open Ethics."

7 In asserting the existence of such attitudes, I speak from long experience as a journalist, newsroom bureau chief, and ethicist connected to several code revision projects, such as the 2014 revision of the code of the Society of Professional Journalists in the USA.

8 At www.reuters.com/backstory

9 However, there is a new national media council in Canada which consolidates pre-existing provincial councils which were struggling or had ceased to operate. At http://mediacouncil.ca.

10 At www.thestar.com/news/canada/2017/10/01/that-rotten-stench-in-the-air-its-the-smell-of-deadly-gas-and-secrecy.html

11 For an example of engaged online journalism, see www.civilbeat.org supported by Pierre Omidyar, founder of eBay.

12 See, for instance, the International Consortium of Investigative Journalists at www.icij.org/about/.

13 They can, for example, use diversity-encouraging sites such as www.readacross theaisle.com.

6 Shape of a future ethic

At the start of this book, I defined journalism ethics as the study and application of norms for responsible practice. Most of the book has been about the application of norms and how they need to change. Yet, journalism ethics also has its theories, scholars, methodological approaches, journals, and conferences. Its scholars, sometimes called media ethicists, are influenced by work in the related disciplines of journalism studies and communication theory as well as by work in ethics, the humanities, and the social sciences. In this chapter, I consider the implications of the disruptions over the past five chapters for journalism ethics as a field of study.

I approach the task in a normative and future-orientated manner. I imagine the shape of a future journalism ethic, if the ideas discussed were implemented in theory and practice. I imagine what a future journalism ethic *ought* to look like, extrapolating from current trends. This imagining summarizes the book.

Figure 6.1 is a look at the future of journalism ethics from 36,000 feet. The big picture. The diagram consists of two rectangular boxes: a large box called global media ethics provides background for the entire diagram. Inside this box is a box that represents my conception of global journalism ethics. This box-within-a-box arrangement underlines my prior remark that journalism ethics is a field of study within a broader communicative ethics.

I divide the smaller box, global journalism ethics, into six topic areas and the arrows point to my perspective in each area. For example, under "approaches" I favor globalism and contractual naturalism, and so on for the other five categories. The three small boxes at the bottom of the diagram belong to global media ethics.

I explore, briefly, the six areas over three sections. I will not re-explain terms from previous chapters. However, I explain new ideas.

Section 1: approach and methods

By "approach," I mean what one thinks about ethics, your ethical mindset. Typical questions include: What are we doing when we do ethics? What function does ethics serve? To what degree are ethical claims objective?

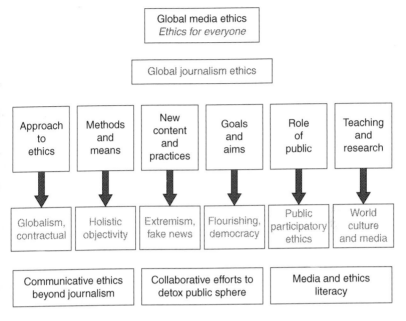

Figure 6.1 Shape of a future ethic

The question for journalism ethics is: What mindset is best?

I have said I support a view of ethics that I call contractual naturalism. It thinks of ethics as the entirely natural (and social) process of seeking agreement on norms for social cooperation. Ethical claims are not descriptions of moral facts but pragmatic proposals on how to coordinate conduct and resolve disagreements. I base those norms on global values, i.e., globalism.

Imperfectionism

I now add this: the epistemology of a future ethic should be what I call "imperfectionism," which adapts ideas from philosophical pragmatism.[1] Imperfectionism is committed to fallibilism and experimentalism. Fallibilism is the view that there are no "metaphysical guarantees to be had that even our most firmly-held beliefs will never need revision."[2] Our beliefs are proposals (hypotheses) on the best way to understand a phenomenon or proposals on the best way to regulate conduct. Fallibilism is not extreme skepticism. It does not require us to doubt *everything*. It only requires us to be ready to doubt *anything* – if good reason to do so arises. Fallibilism rejects the pervasive metaphor of absolutism that our beliefs need infallible, foundational principles, the way a house needs a strong and unmoving foundation. Fallibilism prefers the metaphor of knowledge as on-going inquiry, like a ship already under sail. As we sail along, some beliefs strike us as questionable. We use some of our beliefs to question other beliefs. But we can't question all of our beliefs at the same time.[3] Moreover, we always inquire from *some* type of ship, i.e., a context that includes conceptual schemes and a particular historical period.

Fallibilism dovetails with my view that all inquiry consists of interpretations, and my commitment to experimentalism in all walks of life. If our beliefs are fallible, they can be improved by new experiences and discourse with others. We are psychologically open to new ideas. Even social patterns, such as democracy, are what Mill called "experiments in living."[4]

Imperfectionism is well suited to the imperfect project of constructing a new journalism ethics where ethical norms need to be formulated in an experimental manner, across borders. In a global, plural world, we need an epistemology that promotes a view of inquiry as imperfect and rightfully contested. The attitude encourages us to learn from others, and to enter into dialogue. Rather than look for absolute foundations amid the winds of change, we should work through a global discourse that compares ethical frameworks and is ready to revise. The task of ethics is not to preserve and protect, but to reflectively engage the future with new ideas, new tools.

The social nature of imperfectionist inquiry supports the view that *there is no such thing as a personal or private journalism ethics*. Individuals have journalism values but the justification of those values cannot be subjective – whatever I happen to believe or prefer. The justification must be public. It must show how those values promote important public goals, such as egalitarian democracy. Journalism has an impact on others, hence the need for social justification. This blocks the idea that bloggers, users of Twitter, or anyone who engages in journalism are free to make up their own idiosyncratic ethics, or not bother with ethics at all. Journalism ethics does not "belong" to journalists or individuals. Journalists have no special authority to announce, *ex cathedra*, their personal values as their ethic. Journalists must face the tribunal of the public, not just their own conscience, when their conduct comes into question. They need to provide reasons that other citizens would accept, from a public point of view.

Method: discourse and objectivity

What general methods fit an imperfectionist ethic? If we face a fragmented journalism ethics that requires a radical reboot, then there is one method that is attractive: ethics as a process, a discourse in search of agreement on norms.[5] We should conceive of journalism ethics as a fair, open-ended, and cross-cultural discourse about the norms of digital, global media. Creating this discourse is a major function of journalism ethics.

Ethical discourse converses about values, judgments, issues, and the propriety of certain ways of acting. It is a distinct form of conversing. It is a "give and take" in communication that aims to improve the views in question. Discursive ethics asks participants to engage in a dialogue that honors certain norms of communication – norms quite similar to the norms of egalitarian public discourse. Participants strive for a fair, informed, reasonable, and inclusive "thinking together." Discourse is valued in itself. By discoursing we affirm the rationality and dignity of ourselves and others. At the heart of discourse ethics is evolution, enrichment, and fair negotiation. Discourse ethics believes in the transformative role of cooperative discourse in revising our beliefs and influencing conduct. Discourse ethics is the exploration of an ethics-to-be-formulated, an ethics better able to deal with new conditions.

Ethics as discourse rejects the notion of ethics as pre-established ethical content – a set of static principles handed to humans by God or Nature. This is a view held by many hierarchical religions and philosophical traditions. Absolute principles are to be applied in uniform ways across space and time. An evolving discourse is of minor value. Why discourse at length if we already know the answers? At best, discourse is used to teach the principles.

What is the relationship between dialogic discourse and journalism ethics? First, the idea of ethics as discourse, rather than fixed content, is crucial in an era where journalism is rapidly evolving. If there is no consensus on content, new principles and norms of practice need to be created through discourse. No single authority exists that can "legislate" the content of digital journalism, imposing it on professional and citizen journalists. Therefore, the best option is an open, democratic discourse among journalists and the public. Second, ethics as dialogic discourse is the best option for a global journalism. Digital ethics needs norms that cross borders and can gain the assent of journalists in different media cultures.

Discourse ethics is the best method for seeking agreement on new norms. But we also need methods for actually doing journalism. For practice, I said journalists should redefine themselves as advocates of egalitarian democracy – democratically engaged journalism – while rejecting the methods of both neutral stenography and partisan journalism. Engagement should be objective in method, adopting the techniques and stance of holistic (or pragmatic) objectivity.

Section 2: new content and practices

To create a future ethic, we should create new (fallible) content for codes of ethics and ethical guidelines. We have seen how we need norms for fake news and extreme speech.

New content

Development of new norms should be part of a systematic reform of journalism ethics.

To overcome the fragmentation of journalism ethics we need a new framework that unites diverse practitioners under common values. There should be integration in two domains: digital integration – norms applying across media platforms – and global integration – norms applying across borders. To forge a consensus, principles should be formulated to allow variation in interpretation and application. For example, ethics can allow investigative journalists, daily reporters, and social media journalists to differ on how they honor the principles of truth-seeking and verification, within reasonable limits. Also, ethics must allow the global and the local a voice in reform. Media systems from Canada to South Africa will define differently what they mean by serving the public or the social responsibility of the press. The structure of journalism ethics is less hierarchical and unified than, say, the ethics of the Roman Catholic Church with its infallible Pope and central teachings. Instead, what responsible journalists in different regions of the world may share is an overlapping consensus on basic values such as truth-telling and acting as a watchdog on power and injustice.

We need norm development in at least three areas:

> *Ethics of new media ecologies and new media:* we need guides for practice in new forms of media technology and new forms of journalism, from norms for using social media to norms for non-profit newsrooms.
>
> *Ethics of interpretation and opinion:* journalism will continue to become more interpretive and engaged. We need deep discussions of what norms can guide such writing. What distinguishes good and bad opinion writing? Good and bad interpretations?
>
> *Ethics of global democratic journalism:* global journalism ethics needs continuing work on its aims and how it reports on global values.

Reforming codes

Today, there is much revising of codes, from the BBC to the Society of Professional Journalists in the USA. The Canadian Association of Journalists has developed guidelines for issues such as picking up stories from social media. Some, like myself, have written a global code for journalism.[6]

Multi-leveled codes

Future codes of ethics should have at least three levels:

> Level 1: general principles expressing what every responsible journalist should affirm insofar as they serve the publics of egalitarian democracies.
> Level 2: more specific norms that fall under these principles, plus case studies and examples of how the norms of Levels 1 and 2 apply to daily journalism, such as how to minimize harm.
> Level 3: norms for the leading edges of journalism where new practices cause controversy or debate. This level would be a work-in-progress.

Codes should be dynamic, interactive, and useful. Principles and practical guidelines should be interwoven. Instead of being a list of abstract principles, codes should be living documents with links to sections on new practices and controversial issues; plus guidelines for new technology such as use of drones and virtual reality; plus best practices for vetting information from citizens. Rather than being "ethical eye candy" tacked to a wall or website, codes should be used daily in decisions and improved through public discussion. They should articulate values for both staff and public, and they should be the basis for accountability mechanisms in newsrooms.

Section 3: accountability and teaching

Open ethics

As noted, the digital revolution has given birth to an ethics discourse that goes beyond the confines of media professions. It also transcends borders. The public participate directly in the discussion of journalism ethics. This global discourse, whether angry or restrained, reflective or reactionary, misinformed or erudite, is participatory moral reasoning in the form of public discourse. Unlike many professional discussions, it is informal and unstructured. It mixes together a stew of fact, rumor, bias, interpretation, and ideology. Normative interpretations of journalism conflict. Digital media ethics, at this level, is contested, evolving, cross-cultural, and never settled.

For those who favor systematic thought and careful reflection, this discourse is frustrating and "goes nowhere." For those who favor inclusive, freewheeling discourse, this form of ethics is stimulating and challenging, and much needed. Whatever one's preferences, this is a form of discourse that researchers and ethicists in digital media ethics need to study and understand, because it is the new global forum for journalism and media ethics.

Public participation

As part of open ethics, journalism ethics should be characterized by public-participatory ethics where citizens play a significant role in articulating the ethics of its media, from debating new norms to participating in code revisions and media councils. The news media need to strengthen accountability systems, yet the public also needs to be accountable for its uses of media. Public knowledge of journalism ethics will be raised to a higher level by society-wide collaborations.

Also, journalism ethics is becoming, increasingly, a form of social activism. Today, the critics can join the media players on the field. They can do "media ethics activism." One sense of that term is summed up in the phrase: "If you don't like the media you're getting, create your own media." Media ethics goes beyond criticism. We can create new and counter-balancing media spaces committed to ethical ideals.

Global teaching

The media revolution has changed how schools teach journalism and communications. But what does a disruptive revolution in ethics imply for teaching?

Global journalism implies that schools need to get closer to disciplines that study society, history, and world culture, such as the social sciences and cultural studies. Journalism schools or journalism programs could be linked to disciplines that deal with our global world, such as centers of international communication, the study of global democracy, the anthropological study of other cultures, and the comparative study of religion. Many journalism programs focus on new technology, from data analysis to social media, but such skills should be enriched by a knowledge of the world. Journalists should be interpreters of cultures, deeply aware of their world, its history, and its philosophies. Teaching also needs to incorporate non-Western media theories and interpretations of practice.

We need a new generation of journalists who can mount a resistance to the "mind warfare" of ideological fanatics. We need to educate journalists who can place isolated facts into meaningful context. We need journalists who are at home in the world of policy, culture, and global affairs – cosmopolitan journalists of broad mind.

Global programs are being created. For example, Oxford University and University of Cape Town have developed a master's degree in global journalism. Students spend half their time in London and half in Cape Town, and write about the similarities and differences in media and culture. At University of British Columbia's School of Journalism, they have a global reporting center that takes senior students each year to foreign countries to write a series on some global issue, such as the treatment of mental illness in India. Prior to the trip, the students spend a term learning about the cultures they will be visiting. Academics, and people who live in these countries, help the students understand the issues.[7]

Global journalism ethics is already an established area of inquiry, with books, conferences, and projects aimed at broadening journalism ethics.[8] Ideas are developing in many areas. New books with norms for reporting on human rights are being published. The *Ethical Journalists Network* (EJN) in London is developing norms for covering terrorism, hate speech, and immigrants.[9] EJN has partnered with media organizations in different parts of the world to launch a campaign called, "Turning the Page on Hate." It helped stage a meeting of African journalists in Kigali in April 2014 on the 20th anniversary of the Rwandan genocide to educate journalists on how to avoid spreading hate speech. Subsequent workshops and training have been held in South Africa, Tanzania, Kenya, Nigeria, and Uganda. In June 2016, journalists and academics from China, Japan, South Korea, and the Hong Kong Baptist University met in Hong Kong to create an East Asia Media Forum. The forum produced a glossary of hate speech terms to avoid in reporting. The forum seeks to promote dialogue and media cooperation in a region where the media of each country attack each other, raising political tensions.

Conclusion

The message of this book is: journalism ethics should become a new, more complex, and conceptually deeper, global ethics for responsible communication. Journalism ethics will remain relevant if it conceives of journalists as engaged advocates for humanity and develops norms to guide interpretive journalism. The new ethics will be part academic study, part advocacy, and part application to practice.

You may ask: in the face of journalism's many practical problems, why do I stress mindsets, ideas, and ethics? Why hang on to notions of rationality and objectivity?

Because in the end, so much depends on how we think and value.

This book calls for a discipline of mind that distinguishes between reason and unreason, between seeking evidence and wishful thinking; between being informed and simply *having* an opinion; between being open to revision and being dogmatically self-satisfied; between seeking dialogue and rejecting compromise as a weakness; between the hard road of constructing well-evidenced positions and the easy pleasures of ranting; between welcoming dissent and seeing people with different views as traitors; between communication aimed at richer understandings and communication aimed at rhetorical victory through any means.

When we ask journalists to step back from their own beliefs, to verify claims, and to fairly represent viewpoints, and now to adopt a global view, we ask them to practice their craft in a manner essential to tolerant, plural democracies. This attitude is essential to correcting a corrupted public sphere where it seems that the force of personality and intolerant certainty is all, an illusionary and machoistic sign of strength.

If this mindset prevails, it will surely be the death of democracy and the rise of a new tyranny.

Notes

1 On this philosophical tradition, see Albrecht, *Reconstructing Individualism*.
2 Putnam, *Pragmatism*, 21.
3 The metaphor of inquiry as a ship was popularized by Quine, *Word and Object*, 124.
4 Mill, *On Liberty*, 65.
5 Discourse ethics has been a defining aspect of much contemporary moral theorizing due to the influence of Rawls and Habermas. Rawls, in *A Theory of Justice*, argued that the principles of justice were to be chosen by representatives of groups in a hypothetical social contract. Habermas's discourse ethics, in *Moral Consciousness and Communicative Action*, stressed fair and equal deliberation in ethics and in democracies.
6 At http://mediamorals.org/introducing-the-ward-code-for-global-integrated-ethics.
7 See http://globalreportingcentre.org/.
8 See Ward, *Global Media Ethics: Problems and Perspectives*.
9 At http://ethicaljournalismnetwork.org/en.

Bibliography

Albrecht, James M. *Reconstructing Individualism: A Pragmatic Tradition From Emerson to Ellison*. New York, NY: Fordham University, 2012.

Appiah, Kwame A. *Cosmopolitanism: Ethics in a World of Strangers*. New York, NY: Norton, 2006.

Ayer, Alfred J. *Logical Positivism*. New York, NY: The Free Press, 1959.

Bacon, Francis. *The New Organon*, Lisa Jardine and Michael Silverthorne (eds.). Cambridge: Cambridge University Press, 2000.

Baldasty, Gerald. *The Commercialization of the News in the Nineteenth Century*. Madison, WI: University of Wisconsin Press, 1992.

Batsell, Jake. *Engaged Journalism: Connecting With Digitally Empowered News Audiences*. New York, NY: Columbia University Press, 2015.

Boersema, David. *Philosophy of Human Rights*. Boulder, CO: Westview Press, 2011.

Boylan, Michael. *Natural Human Rights: A Theory*. Cambridge: Cambridge University Press, 2014.

Campbell, Joseph W. *Yellow Journalism: Puncturing the Myths, Defining the Legacies*. Westport, CT: Praeger, 2001.

Cohen, Joshua. *The Arc of the Moral Universe and Other Essays*. Cambridge, MA: Harvard University Press, 2010.

Darwall, Stephen (ed.). *Contractarianism/Contractualism*. Malden, MA: Wiley-Blackwell, 2003.

Datson, Lorraine and Katharine Park. *Wonders and the Order of Nature*. New York, NY: Zone Books, 2001.

Dewey, John. *The Public and its Problems*. Athens, OH: Ohio University Press, 1954.

Dewey, John. *Experience and Nature*. New York, NY: Dover Publications, 1958.

Dewey, John. *Democracy and Education*. New York, NY: Touchstone, 1997.

Dewey, John. *Reconstruction in Philosophy*. Mineola, NY: Dover Publications, 2004.

Dworkin, Ronald. *Law's Empire*. Cambridge, MA: Harvard University Press, 1986.

Dworkin, Ronald. *Sovereign Virtue*. Cambridge, MA: Harvard University Press, 2000.

Freeden, Michael. *Ideology: A Very Short Introduction*. Oxford: Oxford University Press, 2003.

Fuchs, Christian. *Digital Demagogue: Authoritarian Capitalism in the Age of Trump and Twitter*. London: Pluto Books, 2018.

Galison, Peter. "Aufbau/Bauhaus: Logical Positivism and Architectural Modernism." *Critical Inquiry*, Vol. 16, No. 4 (Summer 1990): 709–752.

Gentry, William C. *A Philosophical Life: The Collected Essays of William C. Gentry*. New York, NY: University Press of America, 2008.

Gert, Bernard. *Common Morality*. Oxford: Oxford University Press, 2004.

Ghosh, Dipayan and Ben Scott. "Digital Deceit." *New America Report*. January 2018. www.newamerica.org/public-interest-technology/policy-papers/digitaldeceit. Accessed February 5, 2018.

Goodale, Mark and Sally Engle Merry. *The Practice of Human Rights*. Cambridge, MA: Cambridge University Press, 2007.

Goodman, Nelson. *Languages of Art*. Indianapolis, IN: Hackett Publishing, 1976.

Haack, Susan. *Manifesto of a Passionate Moderate: Unfashionable Essays*. Chicago, IL: University of Chicago Press, 1998.

Habermas, Jurgen. *Moral Consciousness and Communicative Action*, Christian Lenhardt and Shierry Weber Nicholsen (trans.). Cambridge, MA: MIT Press, 2001.

Hayden, Patrick (ed.). *The Philosophy of Human Rights*. St. Paul, MN: Paragon House, 2001.

Ignatieff, Michael. *Blood and Belonging: Journeys Into the New Nationalism*. New York, NY: Farrar, Straus, Giroux, 1993.

Kant, Immanuel. *Groundwork of the Metaphysics of Morals*. Cambridge: Cambridge University Press, 1998.

Kuhn, Thomas S. *The Structure of Scientific Revolutions*. Chicago, IL: University of Chicago Press, 1962.

Levitsky, Steven and Daniel Ziblatt. *How Democracies Die*. New York, NY: Crown, 2018.

Lewis, Clive S. *The Abolition of Man*. New York, NY: Harper One, 2015.

McNair, Brian. *Fake News: Falsehood, Fabrication and Fantasy in Journalism*. London: Routledge, 2017.

Mill, John Stuart. *On Liberty and the Subjection of Women*. London: Penguin, 2006.

Mindich, David. *Just the Facts: How "Objectivity" Came to Define American Journalism*. New York, NY: New York University Press, 1998.

Nathanson, Stephen. *Patriotism, Morality, and Peace*. Lanham, MD: Rowman and Littlefield, 1993.

Nussbaum, Martha C. "Patriotism and Cosmopolitanism." In *For Love of Country*, Joshua Cohen (ed.), 3–17. Boston, MA: Beacon Press, 1996.

Nussbaum, Martha C. *Upheavals of Thought: The Intelligence of Emotions*. Cambridge: Cambridge University Press, 2008.

Nussbaum, Martha C. *Political Emotions: Why Love Matters for Justice*. Cambridge, MA: Harvard University Press, 2013.

Ortega y Gasset, Jose. *Meditations on Quixote*. Urbana, IL: University of Illinois Press, 2000.

Putnam, Hilary. *Pragmatism*. Cambridge, MA: Wiley-Blackwell, 1995.

Putnam, Hilary. *The Collapse of the Fact-Value Dichotomy and Other Essays*. Cambridge, MA: Harvard University Press, 2002.

Quine, Willard V. O. *Word and Object*. Cambridge, MA: MIT Press, 1960.

Quine, Willard V. O. *Pursuit of Truth*. Cambridge, MA: Harvard University Press, 1990.

Rawls, John. *A Theory of Justice*. Oxford: Oxford University Press, 1992.

Rawls, John. *Political Liberalism*. New York, NY: Columbia University Press, 1993.

Sardoc, Mitja. *Handbook of Patriotism*. Basel: Springer International Publishing, Forthcoming 2019.

Sayre-McCord, Geoffrey. "Contractarianism." In *The Blackwell Guide to Ethical Theory*, Hugh LaFollette (ed.), 247–267. Malden, MA: Wiley-Blackwell, 2000.

Schudson, Michael. *Discovering the News: A Social History of American Newspapers*. New York, NY: Basic Books, 1978.

Sen, Amartya. *The Idea of Justice*. Cambridge, MA: Harvard University Press, 2009.

Tolstoy, Leo. *Writings on Civil Disobedience and Nonviolence*. Philadelphia, PA: New Society.

Viroli, Maurizio. *For Love of Country: An Essay of Patriotism and Nationalism*. Oxford: Clarendon Press, 1996.

Ward, Stephen J. A. *Global Journalism Ethics*. Montreal: McGill-Queen's University Press, 2010.

Ward, Stephen J. A. *Ethics and the Media: An Introduction*. Cambridge: Cambridge University Press, 2011.

Ward, Stephen J. A. (ed.). *Global Media Ethics: Problems and Perspectives*. Malden, MA: Wiley-Blackwell, 2013.

Ward, Stephen J. A. *The Invention of Journalism Ethics: The Path to Objectivity and Beyond*. 2nd ed. Montreal: McGill-Queen's University Press, 2015.

Ward, Stephen J. A. "The Moral Priority of Globalism in a Digital World." In *Media Ethics and Justice in the Age of Globalization*, Herman Wasserman and Shakuntala Rao (eds.), 23–42. Houndmills: Palgrave/McMillan, 2015.

Ward, Stephen J. A. *Radical Media Ethics: A Global Approach*. Malden, MA: Wiley-Blackwell, 2015.

Ward, Stephen J. A. *Ethical Journalism in a Populist Age*. Boston, MA: Rowman and Littlefield, Forthcoming, Fall 2018.

Ward, Stephen J. A. "Journalism Ethics in a Digital Era." In *The Handbook of Journalism Studies*. 2nd ed., Karin Wahl-Jorgensen and Thomas Hanitzsche (eds.). New York, NY: Routledge, Forthcoming.

Ward, Stephen J. A. *Objectively Engaged Journalism*. Montreal: McGill-Queen's University Press, Forthcoming.

Ward, Stephen J. A. and Herman Wasserman. "Open Ethics: Towards a Global Media Ethics of Listening." *Journalism Studies*, Vol. 16, No. 6 (2015): 834–849.

Wardle, Claire and Hossein Derakhshan. "Information Disorder." *Council of Europe Report*. October 2017. https://rm.coe.int/information-disorder-report-november-2017/1680764666. Accessed February 5, 2018.

Index

Note: Page numbers in italic indicate a figure on the corresponding page.

Printed in the United States
by Baker & Taylor Publisher Services